REAL MEN LIKE VIOLENCE

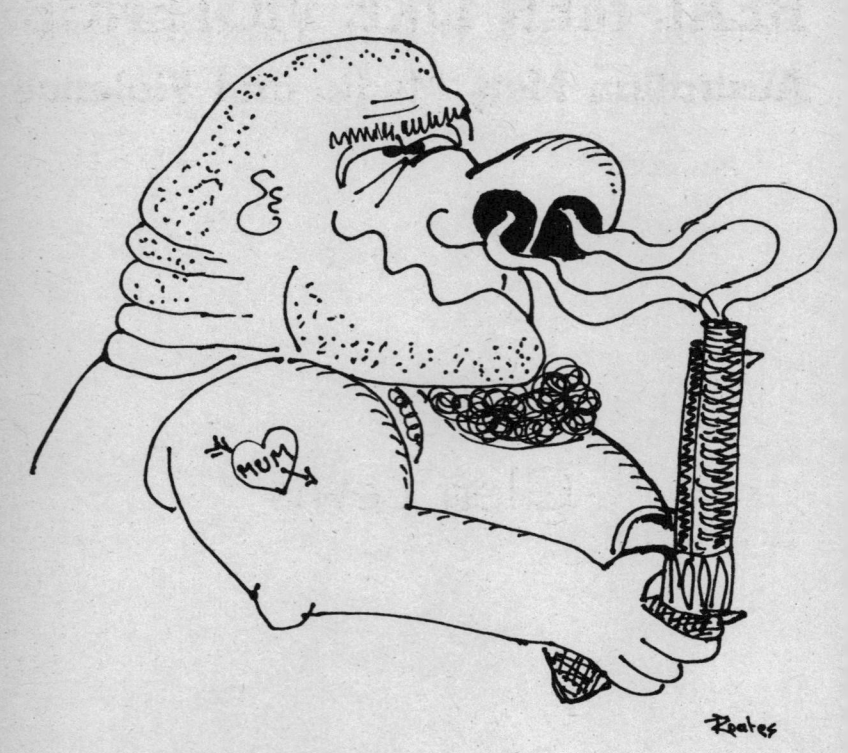

REAL MEN LIKE VIOLENCE
Australian Men, Media and Violence

Glen Lewis

Kangaroo Press

Dedication

For Richard, George, Wally, Andy, and Bill

Acknowledgements
Three of the chapters were previously published as follows: Chapter 2 in *Overland* December 1981, 10 in *Island Magazine* June 1982, 11 in *Australian Quarterly* Spring 1982. Chapter 3 was originally presented at the ANZAAS Conference in 1982.

© Glen Lewis 1983

First published in 1983 by Kangaroo Press
3 Whitehall Road (P.O. Box 75) Kenthurst 2154
Typeset by GT Setters Pty Limited
Printed by Hedges & Bell, Maryborough Victoria

Lewis, Glen, 1943–.
   Real men like violence.

   Bibliography.
   Includes index.
   ISBN 0 949924 55 5.

   1. Violence – Australia. 2. Men – Australia –
   Attitudes. 3. Masculinity (Psychology).
   4. Mass media – Social aspects – Australia.
   I. Zoates, Toby. II. Title.

303.6'2

Contents

Preface 6
1 Talking About Men and Violence 9

Channel 1
2 Rockmen—Angus Chucks a Browneye 21
3 The Kings of Sydney Talkback Radio 28
4 Sportsmen 39
5 Men and Anti-Gay Repression 50

Channel 2
6 Single Men—Loneliness, Love and the Media 61
7 Anti-Social Sex and the Media 72
8 Family Men—Men and Family Life 82
9 Australian Families and the Media 92

Channel 3
10 Starmen—Oz Rock 'n' Role Fantasies 105
11 Militarism in the Australian Media 111
12 Men at Work 120
13 Work and the Media 129

14 Men, Media and Violence 143
15 Alternatives 165
References 170
Index 174

Preface

> Where are the studies of middle- and upper-class men?
> Phyllis Chessler *About Men*, 1977

This is a book about Australian men, media, and violence. Its main concern is to examine the cultural communication of male identity and violence in Australian society and the media. I have tried to walk an intellectual tight-rope between popular journalism and academic analysis, which is hard—and perhaps even impossible—to do. Where I've had to choose between simplification and abstraction I've settled for being straightforward. Readers who are not so interested in the theoretical argument should skip Chapter 1 and read on, while those who want theory should look most closely at Chapters 1 and 14.

My involvement in these subject areas goes back some ten years. In the early seventies I was working at Queensland University in history, and writing about violence in Australian history. At that time I was also strongly influenced—overwhelmed, really—by the impact of feminism on my own marriage and personal life. I've finally brought these issues together intellectually by using the media instead of the past as subject matter. At one level, the book can be read very much as a slice of contemporary history.

Though the book consistently uses the media as subject matter, I have also written at some length about men's experiences in non-media contexts. After teaching media studies for some years, I'm convinced the worst mistake media teachers can make is to separate the media off from society artificially, as if they're a world of their own. If we forget that the media are production organisations in their own right, and that they are the heart of cultural communication in industrial societies, we risk separating the media from their social context—which is just what they do so often in dealing with complex subjects. This is a book which is not so much about the media as one written through them.

I consider European critical theory is the most valuable perspective for Australian intellectuals to use in distancing themselves from the American and British orthodoxies in the field. Media studies traditionally has been dominated by empirical research where blocks of content or audiences are subjected to detailed quantitative analysis. Methodologies are only as good as the people who use them, but I have intentionally used a historical-cultural approach which I think better suited to dealing with the issues under consideration. Some of the material—less than a third—has been published previously, and I have decided to leave this as it stood as an indication of earlier formulations of my main arguments.

In particular, I have placed great emphasis on identifying the recurrent cultural patterns in media imagery. For the first five years I lived in Sydney I was heavily involved in video and film making. This taught me to see the visual media in a different way, and to be more aware of the importance of technical production values and editing methods in producing media meaning. I have tried to carry over my appreciation of the complexity of image construction to my arguments without getting lost in details about differences between media formats.

This book addresses Australian cultural issues, yet most of my media examples are drawn from Sydney sources. There are important differences in the Australian media, between cities and regions, which I don't wish to minimise. On the other hand, Sydney is Australia's largest city, is most directly linked culturally with the U.S., is the centre of Australian film production, and also is a main centre of activity for the Murdoch, Packer, and Fairfax groups. Sydney is increasingly the entrepreneurial centre of Australia. If more ideas come out of Melbourne—and sometimes they do—they are eventually marketed in Sydney.

The types of media I have used most are the popular press and the broadcast media. My main concern is with Australian popular culture, so I have relied most heavily on the media which are grounded in that culture. I have largely excluded film, because so many other writers recently have produced studies of the medium. The greater part of examples used are drawn from media output at the end of 1982 and early 1983, when most of the book was written. I've included some comments on the 1983 Federal election, but have been more concerned with ongoing cultural issues rather than their immediate political setting.

The tone of voice used is often informal, but I've chosen not to be personal. This may be seen as a weakness considering I've so sharply criticised middle-class men for emotional detachment. But I don't believe Australians are likely to be receptive to discussion of these kinds of issues in personal terms. I still hope I've written about the issues involved with genuine commitment.

Last, I want to thank the people who've given me emotional support, editorial advice, and political criticism. Thanks most of all to Sybil, whose warmth and intellectual honesty have been a constant example to me. Thanks to other special women friends—to Trish, Merri, Karen, and Gwenda. Thanks to all the men who've helped, especially to those who talked to me on-camera in 1978/9—Ron, Steve, Ken, Nick, Chris, and even Sasha. Thanks to Paul Kraus and Carl Harrison-Ford. Thanks also to Toby for the cartoons and all the arguments, to Carl Blonde for the good ideas I haven't done justice to, and to Gavin Harris for reading one of the key chapters. I am also professionally indebted to my students and colleagues at Kuring-Gai. Thanks to James O'Brien, Virginia Nightingale, and Harry Irwin. Thanks also to the library students and staff in the School of Library and Information Studies.

But most of all, thanks to the kids—to Morgan and Chloe—who spent a pretty dull Christmas holidays while I was sweating away on this, and for being the awe-inspiringly beautiful individuals that they already are.

G.L.
March 1983

Abbreviations

ADB	Anti Discrimination Board of N.S.W.
AFR	*Australian Financial Review*
B	*Bulletin*
HR	Royal Commission on Human Relationships
M	*Daily Mirror*
NT	*National Times*
S	*Sun* (Sydney)
SH	*Sun-Herald*
SMH	*Sydney Morning Herald*
ST	*Sunday Telegraph*
T	*Daily Telegraph*

1 Talking About Men and Violence

> Today ... the main locus of the internal violence and aggression by which the dominant strata perpetuate their domination has changed position ... this locus is on the plane of intellectual violence and the reduction of activity in the field of consciousness.
>
> Lucien Goldmann *Cultural Creation*, 1976

Is there a link between masculinity and violence? the answer is— probably, yes. There seems to be an historical connection between militarism and masculinism in Western society. More concretely, in postwar years there has been an escalating level of cultural violence. One current sign of this is the re-assertion of tough male roles in the aftermath of feminism—from *Rocky III* to *Mad Max II*. Another is the resurgence of American militarism during the Reagan presidency.

Real Men Don't Talk About Men

Trying to talk seriously about men in Australia today is difficult. Though Australians react quickly to overseas cultural trends, many people don't seem willing or able to talk openly about the issues involved in discussing male identity. So far it's a culturally closeted subject. Treating it on the flippant level of *Real Men Don't Eat Quiche* is too evasive and superficial. Yet talking about men is one thing, and talking about masculinity is another—masculinity is an abstract concept but men are real people.

Looking at the table I'm working on, I can see a random collection of objects that use strong images of masculinity. There's some Kellogs Nutri-Grain with a picture of Grant Kenny as 'Iron Man'. This says that Grant is the first person to ever win both Junior and Senior Iron Man titles. Does this mean all persons are men? Or that women could be Iron Men? Another object on the table is my pack of cigarette tobacco. At Newtown the ad with the usual 'Men Smoke Drum' slogan has been brilliantly graffitied as 'Self Abuse'. Are real men into self abuse? Am I a real man?

Masculinity is arguably one of the great submerged themes of the times, internationally and in Oz. It is a red thread running through football violence, our national preference for patriarchal leadership styles, the prowess of Australian international con-men, the masculine monopoly of the professions, sexual violence—gang rape, poofter bashing, and domestic violence—and symbolically in the macho and paternal stereotypes of 'real men' in the media.

Australian men have two main ways of blocking themselves from talking about masculinity. The traditional way is to write the subject off as women's or poofter talk—this is one major stumbling block men still have to work through. Working-class men also avoid talking about themselves as men because they don't want to appear self-indulgent or big-headed. They're more inclined to let their women speak for them in public.

Middle-class men share some of these barriers, though mediamen—pop stars, celebrities and talk-show hosts— build their careers around their own images as certain types of men. But the more usual way middle-class men avoid the subject of masculinity is by talking about it formally—by putting it at an emotional distance. Middle-class men define the world primarily in rational and formal terms. The language they use in doing this is alternately formal, technical, or political, but each style is grounded in a common element of emotional detachment. I want to try to talk seriously about men and violence in a mixture of plain and formal language. My own class background is mixed, but I've spent most of my working life in academic places. What follows is my attempt to make some preliminary sense about what Australian men really are like today, how we got that way, and what might be done about it. In the absence of much explicit writing on the subject I feel a little like a lunatic explorer, talking about something taboo that Australian men don't seem to want to know about.

Masculinity and Violence

Without precluding other ways of talking about men, I want to define masculinity here mainly via unorthodox American social theory, drawing very freely on Goffman, Klapp, and Sennett. In these terms, masculinity is the presentation of male public and private identity in everyday life.

Male public identity is displayed in politics, in organisations, and in the media; private identity is presented in interpersonal and family relationships, and also in the media. As individuals, men construct their own personal and sexual identities from the range of cultural options generally available in public and private identity. Masculinity can also be thought of in terms of the ways men create space for themselves—social, psychological and emotional space. The more traditional a society is, the more limited will be the range of role options that men can choose from.

Men define themselves and other men mainly through their dealings with each other at work and, second, through their relations with women and children. These roles are formalised in public and family life. Male violence is legitimised in the work-place through the institutionalisation of competitive hierarchies. In social and family life, it is expressed in the maintenance of unequal sex roles. Within certain limits, aggressive male behaviour is accepted as a normal part of everyday life.

Structurally, modern violence is reproduced through the interplay of technology, culture, and identity. Where women historically have specialised in reproducing children, men are specialists in producing the dominant cultural definitions of adult identity. The fathers of the Church were called 'the patocracy', and all the famous early psychoanalysts were men. Male dominance in medicine and psychiatry, and in the military, the police and the media are the modern expressions of this tradition in the sexual division of labour.

Tribal culture in pre-industrial societies was handed down orally through the shamans, chiefs, and tribal elders. Today a swing back is taking place towards the oral transmission of culture through the broadcast media, but this process is impersonal and formalised according to its own set of media production norms. The media have become the main instruments of modern cultural leadership: they are the principal means of communicating public information about technology, culture, and identity.

Technical, symbolic, and personal violence are part of the fabric of daily life in industrial societies. Just as the unequal exercise of political power in dealing with technology reproduces technical violence, inequality in the transmission of media culture reproduces symbolic violence, while the presentation of conventional models of male identity contributes towards personal violence.

There are four main styles of public male identity which men have to choose from. These are related to the unequal distribution of cultural capital and communicative competence between men. In reproducing culture, active male roles are played by technical, official and media men, while working men are left with passive or minor supporting roles. Elite and middle-class men are brought up to expect and assume technical, official and media public roles, but working-class men are brought up to accept their place in the world.

These cultural divisions between men determine their social visibility. In a complex, industrialised mass society the achievement of certain levels of public recognition comes to be a more accurate indication of public worth than the mere possession of wealth. In these terms, technical men can be seen as writers, mediamen as celebrities, and official men as teachers. Working men are students or illiterates.

Regis Debray has argued that the modern intelligentsia is composed of men who are either writers, teachers, or celebrities. His analysis is historically specific to modern France—where the role of intellectuals (and lovers) always has been more visible than in other Western countries. Yet the broad outlines of his thesis can illuminate the experience of other countries as well, even Australia where the intelligentsia has been a much weaker group (Debray, 1981).

Technical men are the modern writers. They deal with cultural authority, where mediamen deal with glamour. Technical men are expected to uphold public standards about the exercise of scientific and industrial power and the allocation of national wealth. Technical men are engineers, scientists, economists, computer workers and systems designers. The scientist is the paradigm of technical man. Mediamen are specialists in entertainment, but technical men specialise in solving problems related to complex physical experience in the real world.

Mediamen are the modern celebrities. It's their job to keep mass audiences entertained. They do this first of all by turning themselves into marketable personalities which can be recognised just as consumers recognise product brand names in a supermarket. Medieval society respected the aristocracy, bourgeois society honoured its own plutocracy—men of wealth and power—while modern society has its mediocracy. In a mediocratic culture information is power and celebrity is an index of social wealth.

Mediamen specialise in dealing with information about personal and cultural experience in public. Mediamen get glamour and money in return for upholding orthodox media standards of self-presentation in public. By doing this they endorse the existing patterns of authority and inequality in society—even if their own image happens to be that of the crusading journalist. Though this is not the way their role is seen by audiences normally, their communication of entertainment is less important than their being orthodox models of personal identity.

Where technical men create information about physical experience, mediamen communicate information about symbolic experience. They also create symbolic information, but their more usual job is to communicate mediated reports about society and culture. Mediamen are media owners and managers, senior journalists, media personalities, and senior advertising and public relations men.

Official men are the modern teachers. They exemplify the publicly accepted male ways of holding and exercising power. Their role-performance criteria are set largely by the vocational norms of the work groups to which they belong. Technical and mediamen can and do also hold official roles, but there are many more official men. Lawyers are the most strategic group of official men, but business magnates and political leaders are the most powerful, while intellectuals, teachers and welfare workers have the least power. Military and police men also play a particularly important part in dealing with the social uses of violence.

The power of individual men in official groups depends on their own place in the national class hierarchy. Elite members of these groups—especially business and political leaders and top professional men—evolve a series of shifting alliances to exercise power and form a political elite. The way personal violence is used depends on the distribution of power between these official male groups.

And working-class men? They are excluded—and exclude themselves—from the performance of active male cultural roles. They may deny, in fact, that the active/passive division suggested here is the right way round, as mental work and cultural creation are disdained in traditional male working-class culture. Mental work is seen as socially inferior to manual work, and is associated with the social inferiority of femininity, while masculinity in working-class culture is linked with action and physical labour.

Masculinity and Sexuality

How men determine their own attitudes to sexual identity can be described in terms of their attitudes to sex, sex consciousness, and sex loyalty (Allen, 1979). How men feel about their own sexual identity decides whether they are orthodoxly male or not, while men's level of sex consciousness decides how aware they are of the level of structured inequality that women experience. Lastly, men's sex loyalties decide whether they are prepared to support women openly and so risk breaking the loyalty bonds between men.

There are four main styles of private sexual identity men have to choose from—conservative, conventional and alternative masculinity, and homosexuality. Conservative and conventional masculinity are orthodox forms of male behaviour, while alternative masculinity and homosexuality are unconventional ways of being masculine.

Conservative masculinity depends on a pre-modern set of cultural attitudes to what real men are. Conservative men are certain of their own sex, have a low level of interest in, and awareness of, women's issues, and a high level of solidarity with other men in supporting traditional sexual values and attitudes. Conventional men, on the other hand, are also certain of their own sex, but have a higher level of awareness about sexual politics. Yet, like political liberals, normally they do not choose to act on these perceptions and passively uphold sexual inequality.

Orthodox masculinity—i.e. conservative and conventional men—reproduces violence in society through its enforcement of sexual inequality. Men who are orthodoxly masculine exist at all social levels, but the media and popular culture are strongly biased in favour of presenting pro-establishment models of male behaviour. The preservation of orthodox masculinity is the basis of interpersonal heterosexual violence. This occurs in real life in rape and domestic violence, while it is supported symbolically through media pornography and sexism.

Modern marriage and living together are in reality often based more on the need for people to form viable partnerships to withstand urban pressures than on the glamour of romantic love. But as divorce rates keep rising and confusion keeps growing about sexual norms, fantasies of sexual violence become more culturally pervasive. Old-fashioned juke-box romance gives way to new-wave bondage fashions, the self-mockery of punk, and the escapist fantasies of the new romantics.

In contrast, alternative masculinity and homosexuality are reactions against the confines of orthodox masculinity. Each postwar generation has produced its versions of unorthodox men—fifties bohemians, sixties flower-children, and seventies punk. Each is eventually co-opted by the dominant culture, but the beats, hippies and punks still succeeded in creating a temporarily free space for personal experimentation, and in some ways changing the dominant culture.

The development of gay society overlaps these movements and also produces men and women who reject orthodox sexuality. The long-term prospects for defusing male aggressiveness depend on the links that can be formed between people in alternative and gay culture, and with those more socially aware conventional men who can see benefits in giving up on the ideal of a rigidly defined male identity. Without the presentation of alternative models of positive identity to choose from, men are left locked into orthodoxly sexist personal roles.

The Media and Modern Violence

The more developed industrial states become, the more they rely on concealed and mediated violence to uphold their authority. When direct violence happens it is represented by statesmen as arising from anti-social criminal elements, or as the result of aggression by foreign powers. Establishment definitions of violence therefore exclude social discrimination as a root cause of violence, and represent social inequality as something eternal, due to individual differences for which the free enterprise state has no social responsibility.

There are three main types of covert modern violence—technical, official, and symbolic. The first two are concealed forms, where their authors deny any intentions of initiating violence. Symbolic violence, on the other hand, is media-generated violence in which mediamen claim to be doing no more than reflecting the troubled condition of society.

Technical violence is based on the exercise of scientific and technical power. Key vocational male groups here are scientists, engineers, academics and intellectuals. The universities remain the main institutional stronghold of technical violence.

Official violence is a result of the exercise of government and corporate power. Politicians, lawyers, company directors and social administrators are the male work roles tied to the exercise of official violence, while government departments and corporations are the main institutional sites of official violence.

Symbolic violence is the result of the power of the media and advertising. Senior journalists, media owners and managers, advertising agents and PR men all deal with symbolic violence, and media and advertising organisations are its main institutional sources.

Where covert violence serves to define societal relations, overt violence is expressed in interpersonal relations. Violent crime, rape and domestic violence are publicly acknowledged as direct forms of interpersonal violence, though with varying degrees of official concern. Social discrimination is the indirect mechanism of interpersonal violence, however. Yet it is denied serious public recognition. Where the state uses the regulation of direct interpersonal violence as a punitive mechanism, its maintenance of social inequality via discrimination is its main long run strategy of class exploitation.

The media create a surreal cultural landscape where men are symbolically defined in terms of orthodox conventions of masculine identity. The media project a series of prototypes (positive ideals) and stereotypes (conventional and negative labels) about 'real men'. The standard TV personality is presented as positive, friendly, amusing and often helpful, where working-class men are presented as stupid, selfish, and violent.

Violence and Australian Cultural History

Australian culture is neither totally independent nor dependent. Australian society always has been interdependent on its overseas sources. The British founded Australia, taking it brutally from the blacks, and native-born Australians since have remained dependent on major overseas powers for their economic survival and cultural identity. Australian technology also has been imported directly from Britain, North America and Europe. Australian intellectuals, artists and cultural workers usually produce simpler Australian versions of mainstream Western concerns after a time-lag.

Though Australian political history is internationally unusual in not having any major internal wars or violent revolutions, the country's social history is also the story of the pioneers' exploitation of both the blacks and the environment. Australian mateship has positive historical dimensions, but the mateship ethos also excluded women, non-whites, ethnics, homosexuals, and the criminal, poor, and mentally ill (Lewis, 1976).

Perhaps the best way of re-thinking the position of Australian culture in the 1980s is to see Australia as an interdependent, provincial society where cultural life has been amazingly fragmented, spasmodic and often rigidly defined on class lines behind a hazy smoke-screen of populism. The worst features of Australian cultural history could be summed up as a tradition of cultural apartheid. The White Australia Policy in the past, and the Fraser Government's 1970s emphasis on a bland, consensual multi-culturalism, are evidence of some of the deep-seated national fears of racial and ethnic differences.

Racial—and sexual—separatism encourages cultural separatism. An often aggressive Australian working-class cultural tradition co-exists uneasily beside an elitist university-based culture today, and both are manipulated by the sensationalism of the commercial media and the official conservatism of the ABC. Regional separation is as important a fact in Australian cultural life as class distinction: Sydney and Melbourne cultural work have concerns of their own which are brought together rarely.

The geographical and historical provincialism and regionalism in

Australian cultural life left the nation particularly vulnerable to the postwar growth of the electronic media. Through the 1970s the media have promoted a homogenised, class-based culture which sells nationalism and aggressive masculinity as moral obligations. All we need to do to cope with world recession, unemployment and social conflict, according to the media, is to keep drinking beer and be real men. 'Why are we here?', asks the Tooth's 1982 summer commercial. Answer: 'We're here for our beer'.

It is because real Australian society is so socially fragmented and divided, and because real Australian culture is so sectarian and insecure, that the commercial media can avoid many significant issues and push nationalism and masculinity as national panaceas. Government-funded advertising campaigns in all shapes and sizes—Do the Right Thing, Keep Australia Beautiful, Declare it for Australia, Life Be in It, etc.—reinforce the media's role in telling Australians there are simple answers to complex problems.

Australian sport also has been ruthlessly exploited to sell patriotism, masculinity, and political images. The ABC, for example, presented ex-prime minister Fraser victorious at the Commonwealth Games in Bjelke-Petersen's Brisbane, while the whole world was supposed to be watching. The event was given unprecedented coverage by a till-then under-funded ABC, but was ignored by the overseas media except for the issue of Aboriginal land rights.

The commercial media have done the same, especially with cricket. The initiative for the Australian communications satellite came first from a Packer-funded research project. The Nine network wanted to use the satellite to beam World Series Cricket across the nation, getting more viewers and reducing the cost of producing Australian drama. Similarly, a 1982 TV ad for the Benson and Hedges sponsored England–Australia series rips off the imagery of *Star Wars*. The stumps and bats are magically turned into laser beams, the cricketers resemble medieval knights, and a pompous voice-over talks about 'a glorious tradition of conflict'. A tradition of conflict is one of the repressed truths of Australian history, but you won't see it on TV.

Militarism and Cultural Devolution

Without falling into the trap of 'prophesying the apocalypse and preaching the need for involvement to prevent it' (Altman, 1979), it seems reasonable to argue that the recurrent crises of postwar Western culture may indicate a movement towards cultural devolution. A search for personal and national survival could be the main cultural theme of the eighties, or even the rest of the century. Just as Darwin's theories about social evolution supplied the main intellectual world view of the last century, a post-Darwininan concern with survival has now re-surfaced.

Cultural devolution can be identified in a number of ways. But what is central to it is the associated development of masculinism and militarism in contemporary American culture, and American economic dominance in transmitting those cultural values to the rest of the Western world. With cultural devolution there is a common process of inversion—going backwards—in technology, identity, and culture.

With technology, public control over the scientific process has been lost. The result is the nuclear balance-of-terror, overpopulation, international poverty, pollution, genetic engineering, and the threat of war. Cultural devolution in technology leads to vocational deskilling in the workplace; in identity it promotes sexual alienation and personal disabling; and in culture it results in the dominance of the media over traditional forms of literacy and interpersonal communication.

And just as a crisis point seems to have been reached in the relation of people to their environment, another has developed in relations between the sexes. In 1973 Suzanne Brogger, a Danish liberal feminist, drew an analogy between the place of the nuclear family and nuclear war in postwar western culture. Her parallel has become more forceful since then. The threat of nuclear war pervades the Western democracies, and this is being used by unscrupulous governments—like Margaret Thatcher's—to progressively erode the civil liberties of its citizens. Meanwhile, the increased reduction of the kinship range of the family has eroded community and social ties.

Some hard-line feminists have argued that the patriarchy benefits all men. I disagree. In reality, there is less of a conspiracy amongst men directed at women, than a social taboo directed against the development of intimacy between men. Men's violence is directed first of all at other men. Yet it is true that men are directly responsible for the military madness of our time. Though the cultural conservatism and political apathy of women are important props to orthodox heterosexuality, female conservatism is no more than the mechanism of privatisation. Masculine aggressiveness is the motor that drives the engine. In contemporary Australian culture *Mad Max* is our own road warrior, the crazy modern inheritor of the bronzed Anzac tradition.

CHANNEL 1

2 Rockmen—Angus Chucks a Browneye

I didn't see the Melbourne AC/DC concert where fifty arrests were reported, but I was one of the more than 20 000 people who crammed into the Sydney Showground the week before to see their eagerly awaited home-town show.

I'm not too sold on big concerts as I get claustrophobia, but this 'Back-in-Black' tour was an historic occasion. It was a kind of Irish wake to honour the recent death of the band's lead singer, Bon Scott. The original Sydney concert had been set for Friday, 28 February, but was washed out, as was the replacement concert the following night. At $12.50 a seat everyone was naturally a little anxious, so when the band announced they'd stay in Sydney till the rain stopped that was great.

One story went that when many kids had vainly queued up on the wet Saturday night they'd got an impromptu invite to go backstage and have a beer with the band. For some of the fourteen-year-olds that must have been a peak experience. It was a characteristic AC/DC gesture too. Generosity and maximum contact with their audience is Side Two of the band's public image. Side One is their nasty, dirty, evil, head-splitting rock 'n' roll music.

The only time I'd seen them before was years ago on TV. Vague memories of Angus Young, the lead guitarist, dressed up outrageously as a uniformed schoolboy in hot, short pants, prancing round the stage of *Countdown*, violently masturbating his guitar while Molly Meldrum mumbled in the background. Those days of schoolboy innocence are gone. Now the band is a major international act which, along with the Little River Band, Air Supply and Olivia Newton-John, is one of the few Australian acts to have made it really big in America. Coming in between the heavy metal bands and before punk, AC/DC retain a massively high-voltage music level which produces some of the loudest, ugliest, and best rock left in an otherwise decadent music scene

Originally published in *Overland*, December 1981.

dominated by disco muzak, new-wave experimentation, and punk pretentiousness.

They are also probably one of the finest performance bands left in the whole rock 'n' role world. AC/DC are the great Oz dinosaurs of the cockrock tradition. Angus has foregrounded his already leading role in the group, and often the whole show stops to highlight his brilliant solos, which are a mix of music, ballet, theatre, mime, and sheer madness. If there is a real warlock left in the rock 'n' roll world it's probably Angus.

When he appeared on stage the crowd flipped out. He was dressed in an exotic, sexually ambiguous costume which retained a touch of the old schoolboy blues, but now looked more like a medieval cavalier's or clown's costume, all crowned with his mop of long unkempt hair with which he whips himself. Painfully thin and incredibly energetic, Angus is a mute star like Chaplin or Keaton. 'Hi, hi, hi', he screamed out once to the crowd in a nervous high voice, but nothing more.

But to really appreciate this entrance it's necessary to backtrack to the start of the show. The security checks were the first thing. The turnstiles were the initial clearance point, then a hundred yards on came a baggage check carried out by bruisers in virginally white T-shirts. The aim here was to keep out drugs and booze, also any sound recording equipment, cameras, or other weapons. Some still smuggled stuff in, but mostly the huge teenage crowd was quite sober and got high just on the excitement and mass claustrophobia.

The grandstands were packed, and as you worked your way carefully towards the front the crowd thickened and got more excited and less friendly. We settled for a spot off to one side of the stage fairly close down. Centre front stage itself was the place for the most determined fans and the drunks, and was where the fights began.

More than anything else the atmosphere was like a huge football match. Most people were standing up and eager to get emotionally involved. During the warm-up groups a vicious routine of exchanges developed between the MC and the crowd, with the obnoxious 2SM DJ alternately whipping the crowd up, then bringing them down by abusing those fighting in the audience. It was commercial and calculatedly callous—the same kind of double-bind behaviorism used in manipulative TV commercials. The fights would stop for a time, some more red hot rock would be piped out to get things jumping again, the DJ would stir the crowd again till another fight started.

This provocation–punishment strategy has come to be normal at many Australian rock concerts. I'd seen Jimmy and the Boys, a neo-Barry Humphries/Kiss group, whip the crowd up and then abuse them for fighting at a big summer concert at Sydney's Castle Hill in

1979. It's this emotional oscillation between excitement and danger which seems to be the main thrill many kids come for. This kind of risk is an integral part of their own collective celebration of themselves and their youth culture, which otherwise is largely excluded by the older ceremonial occasions of Australian public life.

When the first really large pop concerts happened back in the sixties there was frequently an idealism about them, which culminated in the supposed festival of love and peace at Woodstock. Of course there was always an uglier side to it. There were several rapes at Woodstock, and the mass concerts, like the commercial music system they grew out of, were also business operations to make big money. They could and sometimes did turn nasty if the promoters weren't careful to follow the right crowd control tactics. This was what happened at Altamont in California at the Stones' fatal concert.

Still, it remains an awesome experience to be in a crowd of so many excited people. Kerry Packer's World Series Cricket lights brilliantly illuminated the crowd, and it was astonishing to see so many people together at night so clearly. What happens in a crowd of that size is a result of where you choose to go, who you happen to end up next to, and how you behave. There was a fair amount of wariness and curiosity at first, then as the concert warmed up people got stoned on the performance and less aware of those around them. It was then, when the drunks, crazies, and toughs got going, that the nasty side of it all started to come out.

Typically, it's the girls in the audience who get lifted onto their boyfriends shoulders to see, and its the same girls who get hurt when the crowd grows restive and pushy. The guys get into fights, but it's more often the girls who are injured, either by falling from their chivalrous vantage points or as not-necessarily-innocent bystanders at the brawls.

This kind of crowd violence is an integral part of the show—not an unfortunate accidental by-product, as the promoters would claim. There is an implicit violence in both the promoters' management of the concert, as they basically treat their mass audience as profitable, dumb cattle, as well as in the blatant sexism of the band's lyrics and the narcissistic phallicism of their stage performance. AC/DC's songs and stage act are mostly about heterosexual violence. Their songs—like many Top 40 records—are macho variations on an obsessive theme of frustrated romantic love and a complementary sexual fear and hatred of the other partner. So when they get their audience to sing community chorus style—something I remember my parents' generation sometimes doing—the chorus line isn't a statement of love, or peace, or just plain fun, it's 'She's Got the Jack' (clap), which is a vicious piece of sexual politics in its own right.

As well as fostering the illusion of rock 'n' roll as salvation, and viewing romantic love and sexual sado-masochism as good things, there is an implicit worship of technology in these kinds of large pop concerts. The act began with the spectacular descent from above of a giant silver bell, sending out a cavernous electronic boom. This was a moment of pure mad exhibitionism that the crowd loved. This was Hell's Bell, the title of one of their tracks on the new *Back-in-Black* LP, and a salute to the fate of all good rock 'n' roll singers.

Apart from the usual amount of electronic gadgetry on the stage itself, the speaker banks off-stage on either side were at least a hundred feet high. They looked like space modules which had landed specially for the night. This subliminal worship of technology at pop concerts is probably a subconscious recognition of the dominance of the death-oriented, military-scientific complexes in industrial culture, and can be seen as the demonic counterpart to the youth culture's mystical faith in rock 'n' roll as salvation.

Once the music starts, though, these kinds of comment become absurd. Angus' blatantly homoerotic performance was a regularly interrupted series of long, almost oriental, nerve-wrenching guitar solos, climaxed by tortured sonic booms. The musical message was the same as that of 2SM's crowd control tactics—provoke, punish, never completely satisfy. Finally, the high point came when Angus chucked his browneye. It was about two-thirds of the way through. One moment he was near centre stage, close to the end of another tortured, deafening solo; next he was stripping like a seasoned drag star. He took it all off then turned his naked bum on the audience, bent over, and threw a 'v' sign at the crowd—that's chucking a browneye, mum.

And there was more. Disappearing briefly, he re-emerged down in the audience at the side of the stage. This time with his pants on, sitting on the new lead singer's shoulders and still crazily playing his guitar via a remote control pickup. He charged recklessly through the most packed, violent part of the crowd down front, which gave way like the Red Sea for Charlton Heston's Moses. That kind of contact with an audience is exceptional in rock today.

What I've been suggesting is that the regulation of pop concerts today has become a basic part of cultural politics in industrial societies. It is a means for both releasing and reinforcing the emotional energies involved in the state's politicisation of everyday life. As meaningful public communication decreases, the private sphere of everyday life becomes increasingly regulated and controlled.

Concerts this big can be promoted only by large media groups, either record producers, radio stations, or TV companies. In AC/DC's Sydney concert the promoter was 2SM, one of the largest and most culturally visible AM broadcasting groups in Sydney, and sister station to 3XY in Melbourne. The station aims at a teenage–young-adult market and recently ran their own Rock 'n' Roll Eisteddfod, where schools were encouraged to have their students present mimed versions of current 2SM Top 40 material. This strategy is indicative of the dominant–subordinate relation which exists between the media and education systems in Australia today.

Rebellion against school and authority is one of the perennial themes of postwar pop, starting with Chuck Berry's classic 'School Days', and most recently updated by the Pink Floyd hit 'Brick in the Wall'. There is a healthy cynicism about these songs that tell the kids that schoolteachers and school are bad news, and rock 'n' roll is good news. That's a mystical proposition, but an appealing one. Once young people got excited about God and salvation, now salvation is available only on rock 'n' roll records.

These songs reach their audience through a broadcasting system which is as dominated by official culture as the education system is, but it stresses popular instead of high culture and is, necessarily, more impersonal. It is also much more glamorous. The average DJ develops a hyped-up media persona that average teachers can't compete with, and often think beneath their dignity anyway. That is, the media educators are the impersonal at-a-distance role models young people prefer to identify with, while the commercial, competitive, anti-intellectual and sexist values the media gurus stand for are transmitted far more effectively than the curriculum is in schools. One-way communication is most efficient if your main aim is propaganda or persuasion.

So the rebellion and violence that modern pop music plays on is rarely stated in political terms as most teenagers see politics as just one more repressive system like school and work. Punk, with its explicit statements about anarchism and anti-royalism, was the exception here.

Consequently the potential for genuine political violence (even as a riot: 'Who wants to march/When you can riot?' is the lyric of one Sydney punk band) is funnelled off into an obsessive preoccupation with private relationships, mostly sexual ones, and it is this tension which is played on by groups like AC/DC.

Rock bands' expression of their audience's potential for group violence is not communciated to a large crowd, however, except under conditions over which the promoters and the authorities have complete control. When pop crowds turn really nasty the police intervene. This was what happened at the 1979 New Year's Eve 2SM Opera House concert, when the crowd justifiably became violent after being packed in like sardines and subjected to the insults of pseudo-stars like Jon

English and the smarmy patronage of the then Lord Mayor, Nelson Meers. It happened also in Brisbane in the late seventies, where punk was fostering a radical political subculture until the police clamped down. Recently there's been a move to ban large outdoor concerts completely—supposedly the AC/DC show was the last one at the Showgrounds—and smaller places are also harassed if they become too popular. Pubs and clubs like the Grand and the Stage Door in Sydney were closed down for this reason by the police, and their audiences have to go somewhere more commercially conventional.

What is at issue here is corporate control over the definitions and uses of public space. Urban space is a commodity, either for leisure-time activities or real-estate speculation. Just as the streets of Paris were rebuilt in the nineteenth century to preclude barriers being erected across them in an insurrection, the Australian urban terrain today is constructed in such a way as to ensure the maintenance of public order. Seen in this light, commercial public culture in the West today often comes close to a form of officially sanctioned terrorism. At concerts like AC/DC's the crowd is put into a situation where if anyone gets hurt it's going to be them. Though there is a romantic mystique about being a male cockrock star that encourages self-destruction, it probably won't be the band itself or the concert promoters who are injured. It'll more likely be the teenagers from the suburbs—the F. J. Holden crowd—who'll get hurt. And the worst violence is done psychologically. Most of the crowd don't get directly involved in the fights, but all of them pick up on the bad feelings, many enjoy it, and subsequently come to associate emotional satisfaction with sexual provocation, punishment and violence.

This manipulation isn't the fault of rock music itself, which as a social performance can transcend the banal content of most rock lyrics and music. When AC/DC sing 'Rock 'n' Roll Ain't Noise Pollution', the audience gets off because they agree: state regulation and control they don't like, music and fun they do. What makes rock politically backward isn't so much the music, but the anti-social commercial structures in which rock music is contained by media monopolies.

Pop concerts should belong to the people. There should be more parts of public space opened up for sheer enjoyment, which shouldn't be sold out to the highest media bidder. There are alternative ways of organising carnivals, such as the promising Festival of Sydney, but until that space is greatly enlarged big pop concerts will often continue to damage their audience's sense of their own personal worth. This way the public image of AC/DC, instead of standing for a subversive model for bisexuality and liberation—as the term AC/DC first meant—is co-opted into more chauvinist cockrock and more conservative commercialism.

Still, AC/DC's brand of Ozrock has added a new sheen to the aging features of Big Daddy rock 'n' roll, and positively influenced some of the best young bands around. At the recent *Countdown* rock awards, Cold Chisel smashed up the show and mocked compere Molly Meldrum after collecting all the awards. Social protest, in other words, still lives in Australian rock.

3 The Kings of Sydney Talkback Radio

Sydney talkback radio has grown alarmingly in the last few years. Just as Australian TV stations have emphasised news formats, following US models, radio has extended its news and newstalk shows. Yet Australia is not America. The media public is smaller, less educated, and less articulate than American talk show audiences. Australian commercial radio also pays detailed attention to the grimier side of life, but these shows take place in a different cultural setting where an emphasis on aggressive masculinity is often taken for granted.

John Laws, John Singleton, and John Tingle presently occupy the 9 to 12 morning slot on Sydney's talk stations. John Laws' top-rating version is more traditional and less informative than Tingle's, while the Singleton version rarely treats the news systematically, but GB, UE, and KY—as well as BL—are all doggedly pushing morning newstalk formats.

John Laws as Living Legend

John Laws is acknowledged by most journalists to be the reigning king of Sydney radio. *60 Minutes'* recent profile treated him respectfully. It repeated some of the key points of the Laws folklore—his own problems with relationships, his country retreat, and his credibility among his peers. These angles were tied together with a 'public confidence, private agony' punch line about Laws, which was very accurate comment (17 April '82). Laws as a public personality, that is, shows through warts and all, which is a pleasant change from the blandness of many Australian TV and film stars.

Three years ago Laws was publicly notorious for his involvement in the run on the N.S.W. Building Society and the truckies' strike.

Originally presented at the ANZAAS Conference, 1982.

'There's nothing the matter with John Laws,' Craig McGregor wrote in a profile at the time. 'He is personally quite disarming, even likeable. But what he does is grotesque, destructive (including self-destructive), and finally unforgiveable' (*NT*, 24 March '79). Here McGregor left the story hanging. One of Laws' great strengths as a performer is that few of his critics are as confrontational in their style as he is. Considering that Laws recently successfully sued the Fairfax group for unfavourable publicity concerning the use of his name in connection with a real estate scandal, it seems that few Australian journalists can make much serious criticism of John Laws.

Laws puts his personal shortcomings out openly in public. He has expressed concern, for instance, that he's unpleasant to look at. The rich, mellow voice comes out of a rather battered and not-so-confidence-inspiring face. Laws is not at ease on TV (or in print), perhaps because of this. *60 Minutes* also suggested Laws was a tough, rather remote man with few friends. Laws has nine children and thirteen cars. Col Joye, Brian Henderson and John Singleton were said by *60 Minutes* to be Laws' inner circle, and he relies heavily on his wife. Laws himself acknowledged that relationships he had with people didn't last, and that he could give advice about personal relationships but not take it. For their parts, Laws' friends stressed his credibility as a radio salesman. 'He could sell ice cubes to Eskimos', said Singo.

Laws' image, then, is an odd mix of vulnerability and ruthlessness. He projects himself as the sophisticated, macho man of Sydney radio, as well as the last of the silver-tongued cowboys. His personal tastes in music are basically old-fashioned, but he tempers this romanticism with a scathing tongue and cynical comments about people and politics. As the Falkland Islands dispute dragged on, for instance, Laws suggested tongue-in-cheek that a good little war would help Britain get back on its feet and sell records for Vera Lynn. It would save Vera that awful trip from London to the Revesby Workers' Club (26 April '82). This final barb was pure Laws.

Laws as Dole-Bludger Basher

In late March Laws went on a systematic anti-dole bludger campaign with which he is still (late April) persevering. To do this was in line with his own political beliefs. On programme one (24 March '82) Laws delivered an extended sermon on the evils of dole-bludging. This began with scorn being poured on another type of Australian male bludger—

the wife deserter who escaped making social security payments. The government should protect these women and track down the men, claimed Laws, who then linked the maintenance bludgers with the dole bludgers proper. He knew of a man living *in an executive suburb* (Laws' emphasis) getting five dole cheques a week. Laws calculated that if 10 per cent of people on the dole were doing this it was costing Australian taxpayers $250 000 a week.

Laws then attacked the employees of the CES for putting up with abuses in the system. 'You people who work at the CES, you're robbing yourselves. Millions of dollars a year are being torn out of this country. It's insane, unjust, immoral grand larceny.' The core of the problem, Laws concluded, was that we 'are not breeding a race of responsible Australians'. This is the characteristic language of Anglo-Australian conservatism, drawn from horse breeding and eugenics. Laws' main appeal here, as usual in such matters, is couched in terms of moralistic national authority. Laws is not just a nationalist, he is a romantic, moralistic nationalist.

On programme two (1 April '82) Laws claimed that postage costs of dole cheques cost taxpayers $2 million a year, which easily could be saved by the unemployed themselves collecting them. This masterpiece of Lawsonomics—who would pay for the unemployed travelling to get there?—was another angle on the anti-dole bludger campaign. Other highlights were:

10.57 A male personnel officer in an Engineering business calls in support. He claims to regularly get job applications for positions advertised weeks previously. This is done intentionally, he claims, so applicants will not get the job, but still have their interviews recorded to satisfy the work-search requirements of the CES.

11.12 A housewife calls in support. She claims that in New Zealand the unemployed can volunteer to do community cleaning work and get $15 a week. So New Zealand, unlike Sydney, is not a pigsty.

11.25 A housewife calls in support. She claims to know of a man receiving five dole cheques a week under false names.

11.37 John Laws discusses the possible outcome of a referendum to introduce national identity cards. It wouldn't work because too many unemployed would vote against it, so the government should just do it.

Laws finished this particular section by promising soon to get hold of the Minister for Social Security, to ask him 'across the desk—not on the phone' about these abuses.

Laws persuasive strategies in these two programmes are fairly clear. He sets the agenda by complaining vigorously about something, lays down the line for the day, then accepts calls which mostly reflect his own viewpoint. Traditional Australian community prejudices about crime, poverty, and unemployment are triggered by his application of this format to the dole-bludger issue, so he mostly gets the restatement of clichéd views that the unemployed are lazy, dishonest, morally corrupt and criminally inclined.

He constructs speculative figures about the social costs of dole-bludging in terms of millions of dollars, but rarely acknowledges that it is organised and corporate crime in the state which really does business of that order. Laws' show is based around episodes like the anti-dole bludger campaign. Technically, he foregrounds minority group negative stereotyping in his show. Informally, he specialises in moral crusades against the unrespectable weak—the unemployed, prisoners, homosexuals, anti-nuclear demonstrators—in the name of the upright citizen and honest taxpayer.

Laws as Emotional and Cultural Censor

Critics of the media normally have focused on the factual aspects of media distortion of public issues in news programmes. Yet Laws' approach works on several related levels, only the first of which is cognitive. As an approach to the facts themselves there is a consistent selecting of the news by Laws to suit his own attitudes. The medium helps him do this. Radio talk seems to work in patterns of allusive cross-reference. Listening to radio, that is, is more like looking at the whole page of a newspaper than just at one item. If information on TV is presented cyclically, and print linearly, then radio information is presented laterally, with an emphasis on short-term cross-referential associations.

Critically competent listeners can and do cope with the different logical levels of argument and frames of reference used by Laws, but many of his anonymous callers often demonstrate low levels of competence. Laws' style easily creates inferential confusion among his less educated listeners. He casually jumbles up his own logical levels, as highly skilled public speakers can, yet usually retains his bearings. Audiences with lower levels of logical competence cannot do the same.

Second, Laws' method of talking promotes distorted emotional responses. More specifically, it inhibits spontaneous emotional responses. Talkback radio depends on conversation and conflict, yet the listening audience is rarely exposed to examples of extended disagreement, anger, or conflict between talkback hosts, guests, and callers. Just as private behaviour in Australian public places is strongly regulated by prevailing norms of respectability, sobriety and decency, talking and listening on the airwaves is quite inhibited when compared with normal patterns of Australian speech interaction. Real anger is usually excluded from talkback radio, just as is real intimacy—which is even rarer. While TV focuses repetitively on male violence and heterosexual intimacy, neither rage nor intimacy are often heard on radio.

Third, as well as speaking to the logical and emotional ranges of his listeners, Laws speaks to their sense of belonging—their cultural identity. Laws himself is a by-now baroque monument of Oz popular culture, along with a few others like Barry Humphries, Graham Kennedy and Bert Newton. The importance of the media's treatment of popular culture is that it regulates its expression and tends to emphasise its reactionary parts, either to sell products, to reinforce sexist and racist stereotypes, or to bolster the establishment's political dominance.

To claim that Laws' show promotes the limitation of his listeners' emotional range cuts across the common-sense perception of Laws as a trouble-shooter and fighter. But Laws is mostly a shadow-boxer. His own arrogance, rudeness and egocentricity spark off many fights with his listeners, but these scraps with anonymous callers are mostly used as entertainment. While Laws is likely to argue fairly vigorously either with studio guests or callers who represent group viewpoints, he has little time or patience for ring-in listeners with whose views he disagrees.

At the end of programme one on dole-bludgers, for instance, Laws took an angry call from a male listener who resented Laws' approach (24 March '82). This caller detailed other areas of corruption in Australian public life, notably the recent medical frauds and the ongoing curtailment of civil liberties in Queensland, but Laws refused to reflect this caller's anger. He commented instead that individual freedom was OK as long as people didn't abuse it, then cut the call. So faced with a genuinely angry response, Laws is more likely to be dismissive than confrontationist. His difficulty in becoming publicly angry shows through on *Beauty and the Beast*, where his radio reputation for aggressiveness obviously fails to work.

John Tingle—All New 2GB Newstalk 87

John Tingle's 2GB Newstalk 87 is currently the clearest model of an informed commercial Sydney morning newstalk show. Tingle is an experienced broadcast journalist, unlike Laws and Singleton, and has worked in that capacity at the ABC and more recently at 2SM with Brian White and Steve Liebman. Tingle's image is relatively sober and low-key. He projects himself as a concerned citizen and family man, and the 2GB broadcast news promo describes his slot as 'controversial' (24 March '82). Sometimes it is. Other contributing reasons for the high-profile news orientation of 2GB are the station's corporate links with the Fairfax/Macquarie Network news group, and its physical position on the dial, falling between the traditionally news-oriented 2BL and 2UE.

Tingle's show has several good features. First, it pays more serious attention to daily news than most other commercial stations. Like 2UE and 2CH it features a half-hour midday news bulletin, and with Micki de Stoop and Stephen O'Doherty carries its current affairs emphasis through the rest of the day. Second, it gives supportive non-patronising attention to women's issues. The print ad for the show specifically appeals to intelligent women (*M*, 16 March '82). Tingle has conducted some marathon talk-sessions on issues such as rape and abortion. Third, Tingle's show looks closely at a wide range of social issues, such as the environment, religious freedom and racial intolerance. Last, Tingle treats his own role in the show critically from time to time, and directly discusses how he sees the media affecting news and politics.

The negative parts of the show are twisted reflections of its strengths. Tingle is possibly performing as important a public educational service with women's issues as Ita Buttrose did at the *Weekly*, though Tingle's audience is smaller. Another 2GB Newstalk broadcast promo explicitly labels the show educational—citing Independent MLA and Mayor of North Sydney, Ted Mack, who describes the show as a community education service.

Yet though Tingle pays more explicit attention to current women's issues than Laws, his format still breaks these issues up and treats them separately as 'women's issues'. Laws more successfully integrates his comments about women over a range of subject matters, where Tingle tends to change hats in talking about other subjects. Tingle also tends to accept some minority women's group viewpoints uncritically and sometimes treats unsympathetic male callers patronisingly. By doing this Tingle presumably alienates many men listeners. Non-feminist women are excluded or made to feel guilty for not being feminist, while those actively involved are probably dissatisfied with the expression of one solution to the subject.

What reduces Tingle's impact as a hard-hitting reporter is that, by complaining as much as he does about public standards, he falls into the Australian folk tradition of the knocker or whinger. The danger with political criticism made primarily in moral terms, like the reportorial style of John Pilger—who is a Tingle-type personality writ large on TV—is that the main source of such criticism is moral indignation. Australia has a pretty tough political tradition, so moral indignation by itself is unlikely to lead to social change. One caller confronted Tingle with this. Identifying herself as European-Australian, comfortably off, and middle-aged, she stressed the futility of complaining as a means of political reform. Tingle's response was that anyone in a community-responsible function deserves to be complained about if he acts incompetently or corruptly. This was just a re-statement of his own position, not a rationale (24 March '82).

Tingle sees his show as having a definite impact on public opinion. 'We don't want a nation of grumblers and complainers,' he said recently in discussing the show's approach, 'but we take too many things lying down' (24 March '82). John Laws views here are more blunt. 'Australians are the most apathetic and cynical people in the world', said Laws while discussing the media's role with Liberal Opposition Leader John Dowd (14 April '82). Referring to the N.S.W. power crisis and the Easter road death roll, Laws claimed that public opinion on these and other matters was ephemeral. Dowd agreed, adding that the N.S.W. media were good at treating day-to-day issues, but hopeless at covering ongoing matters.

Tingle's views on the role of the media seem less realistic. He sees his radio role as a mild crusader, and because of this tends to exaggerate the power such programmes can command. He reacts oversensitively, for example, to claims of media bias by his listeners. During the press controversy over the seal-killing issue, the Canadian High Commissioner issued a press kit about media bias. Tingle's response was that media bias here wasn't a real issue (24 March '82). Again, during the post-Easter Fraser/Peacock leadership feud, Tingle read out a listener's letter which similarly criticised the media's contribution. Tingle's reaction once more was sheer disbelief, though a minute earlier he had read a news bulletin about the contest which described it in conventionally aggressive terms (7 April '82).

At his best Tingle's approach to public affairs is critical and concerned, but in his bad moments he is superficial and alarmist. In one March programme he ran together fears about the new American religious sects in Australia, fears about electricity bills, and the dangers of parachuting from the Sydney Harbour Bridge (24 March '82). Where Laws takes a paternalist position on most social issues, Tingle speaks as a small-'l' liberal social reformer—he wants to encourage people to help themselves rather than rely on authority. 2UE, for instance, has its own Kids'-Care counselling line, and 2GB has not.

The problem is that as a reformist talk-show host Tingle is the only liberal teacher in a staff room full of conservatives and bullies. His brand of newstalk is at times also too school-masterly for public consumption. Attempting to cover so wide a range of serious issues, the tone of Tingle's show is often doggedly earnest and sometimes carpingly negative. Where Laws growls and Singo grumbles, Tingle complains.

John Singleton—The 2KY Mumbleback Wireless Show

Singleton's mumbleback show with Harry Wilde now has run for more than twelve months. Singleton's show is less of a newstalk format than a series of personal and political ramblings about Singleton's current interest. Racing, football, sex and Harry S. Baggs are the recurrent subjects Singleton warms to. His treatment of current affairs otherwise is sporadic and idiosyncratic. Where John Laws speaks mostly in a parental, confident, opinionated way, Singo presents himself as childishly naive and egocentric. Where John Tingle shifts between a John Normal/Mr Righteous approach to issues, Singleton is alternatively the Larrikin Con-Man and the Good Bloke and Sportsman.

Singleton's version of the *enfant terrible* approach to radio is similar to Laws' but different. Where Laws projects himself as a sophisticated man of the world concerned with serious issues, Singo comes on more as rude, crude, unattractive and obsessed with the latest sports results. Laws is macho, Singo is self-consciously ocker. Singo, like Tingle however, is a minority Sydney radio taste. Though 2KY boosted their ratings after a period of the Casey/Singo format they have currently slumped badly.

Singleton's talkback world deals regularly with women, men and sports as subjects of equal importance. Women are usually cast in traditional roles, men are seen either as friends or enemies, and sports news focuses on gambling, corruption and conflict. Singo's appeal to women is part of his media image. Where Laws and Tingle—especially Laws—project themselves as dedicated family men, Singo behaves more like a bachelor. His recent engagement to Belinda Green—an Australian former Miss World—drew lots of media attention.

Singleton has succeeded in winning over at least some of his female listeners. When Belinda Green took the show over from him late last year, she had a long sympathetic talk with Rebecca, one of Singo's regular callers and a fervent admirer. Belinda agreed to let Rebecca have John to herself on air between nine and twelve daily. Singleton has a penchant for kitsch sentimentality of this kind and often flirts with his women callers. One promo used to open the show featured a suicide call from a woman listener. Singleton had talked her out of her depression, then subsequently replayed the highlights of the conversation as an introductory promo (February '82).

Singleton's dealings with other men on air are less romantic and more rowdy. Singo specialises in sneers and putdowns of men he doesn't like. Where John Laws is likely to be openly rude, Singleton will be snide and evasive. At the same time, he admires and sometimes adulates an odd collection of male cronies—an assortment of sporting, business and assorted low-life male anti-heroes. There are also the powerful friends. Singleton has had Rupert Murdoch on the show calling from New York and often features Joh Bjelke-Petersen. There is a stronger emphasis on male bonding and comradeship in Singleton's format than in either Laws' or Tingle's. Singleton's abrasiveness is directed randomly at his guests, callers, his show co-host Harry Wilde, and his female producer Ros, who is often the butt of Singleton soliloquies.

Ruminating on the personal differences between himself and 2KY's other morning talkshow host, Ron Casey, Singleton concluded by saying 'Ron's got more balls than brains. Good on yer Ron' (4 January '82). The same prejudice and tunnel vision comes through in Singleton's treatment of sexual morality in general, and gay rights particularly. Singleton is willing to put either Fred Nile or Gay Rights representatives on air to entertain his listeners and show them both up as ratbags. After speaking to Nile in March 1982 about the slow progress of the homosexual law reform bill in State parliament, Singleton recalled how 'we had a poof in school once and he got gay-bladed'. This was a reference to the November '81 so-called 'gay blade' murders in central Sydney. Singo's conclusion was that homosexuality should be legalised to make it less attractive. This reflected both his ideological opposition to government, plus his hostility to homosexuals (16 March '82).

Singo's involvement in sport is one base of his media appeal. Horse racing is a perennial topic of the show. Singleton, like other Australian media personalities (Willesee, Pickering, Micki de Stoop), is a horse lover with interests in racing and breeding. This image fits in well with 2KY's country-and-western music format and its heavily racing and football oriented sports programmes. Racing remains one of the most heavily covered radio sports. Singleton's business and social commitments to the Jets, Newtown's League team, are as striking. Singleton has involved himself heavily with the club, probably to his regret when he drew criticism for providing legal aid to some Newtown footballers arrested for drug trafficking in Thailand (*S*, 15 October '78).

Singleton is also a keen boxing fan. He and Laws sponsored Rocky Gattelari's unsuccessful comeback, and Singleton still follows professional boxing. On 2 April 1982 a boxing night at the Opera House was marred by several real brawls, which prompted officials to ban future matches there. The next Monday (5 April) morning on 2KY Singo was jubilant at the level of viciousness displayed in the bouts. This was at the same time that news reports were being made about the need for more police and even vigilante squads in Sydney's western suburbs. In 1979 Singleton himself had been involved in a Kings Cross brawl with plain clothes police (*M*, 1 March '79).

Conclusion: Talkback as Cultural Larrikinism

Few leading radio personalities are one-dimensional. They are usually highly communicatively competent individuals who are voluble, articulate, informed, and have complex sets of values and attitudes. Yet talkback men on Sydney morning radio consistently come through as clear, sharp-edged personality types, especially compared with the blandness of TV personalities.

Talkback radio men focus squarely on the problematic and potentially controversial areas of modern Australian city life. Where TV smooths out personalities, talkback radio highlights them and accentuates their toughness. The results sometimes are bizarre. That there is a rather grotesque dimension to talkback is appreciated by the hosts themselves and others in the industry. When Margaret Throsby was interviewed on the *Mike Walsh Show*, she admitted she didn't much like talkback radio (24 March '82). Used injudiciously it could lead to 'agony calls' and she could do without that. Throsby, however, is a panelist on Laws' *Beauty and the Beast*, which is based on similar principles of audience self-humiliation.

Talkback radio men are the headline setters, the flagship personalities of their stations' news-teams. The kings of talkback become kings by winning public attention and holding on to it. They do this by being the rude boys as well as the kings. Australian TV often projects bland mainstream images of male identity. In contrast, talkback radio acts more as an outlet for traditional Australian male larrikinism.

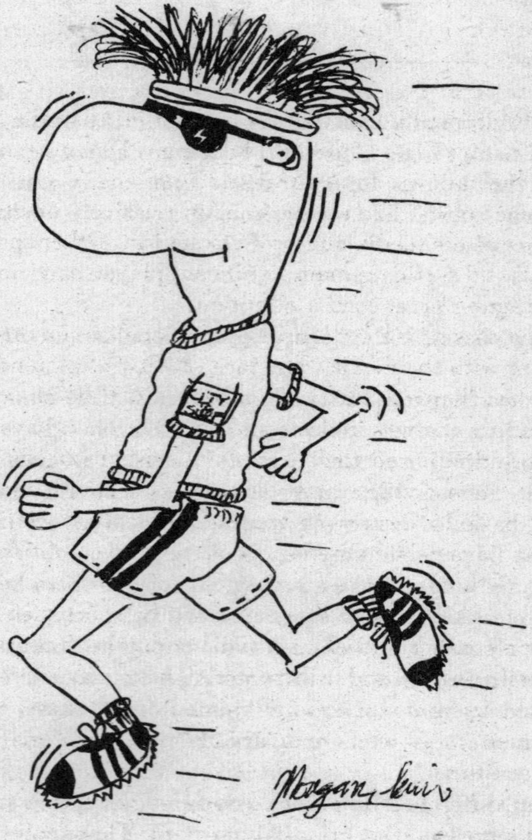

4 Sportsmen

Sportsmen traditionally have been honoured in Australia. Names like Bradman, Cazaly, Clive Churchill, Sedgman, Dawn Fraser and Phar Lap are better known to Australians than many current political leaders'. Some sports, like racing, remain relatively unchanged today by the impact of the media and professionalism. Other sports too, like bowling, golf and surfing remain significant player-participation sports without attracting great media attention.

But the big change is the postwar professionalisation of sport and its entanglement with the media. The face of Australian tennis, football, and cricket has changed drastically as a result. Rule-changes in many sports, including changes in dress and speed of play, have speeded up these sports and adjusted their pace to television's needs. Meanwhile off-the-field sponsorship and advertising have changed their commercial basis by destroying traditional local associations.

The media have personalised sport as they have politics. The sports pages and programmes have a star system of their own headed by the biggest current stars. The values expressed by sportsmen through the media favour conflict and competition, strength of character, determination, self-control, and will power. These masculine virtues are also endorsed by many successful women sports stars, while media sports commentators—who are invariably men—reinforce these values and add their own.

Significant differences in values associated with each sport and the style of media presentation are still important. These point to the effect of long-term changes in community attitudes to sport itself and different sports. Attitudes to violent sport, for instance, in most western countries have hardened since the war. Professional boxing is no longer a socially respectable or commercially viable Australian sport. Violence in sport has not disappeared though, but has been displaced into different areas. The occurrence of physical violence is less common in sport nowadays than the expression of ruthless competitiveness.

Marathon Men

A quite new sense of body and health consciousness developed in Australia in the late seventies. Joggers became a regular sight in city streets, while the City-to-Surf events—sponsored by the *Sun* in Sydney—attract thousands. The 'Life Be In It' campaign capitalised on this trend, with Norm as the TV stereotype of pot-bellied, unhealthy, Australian men. New sports like abseiling, wind-surfing, and hang-gliding share a concern for the expression of individual freedom. Their growth, along with the continuing importance of bowls, golf, and racing express a counter-direction in Australian sporting tastes which runs against the media's incorporation of mainstream sports. Women are an important part of the new sports. In 1982 the N.S.W. state bodybuilding championships included an open women's event, which was splashed on page one of the *Sydney Morning Herald* (22 November '82).

Jogging and long-distance running are model examples of the new individualism in Australian sports. A *SMH* profile of Robert de Castella, Australia's new champion marathon man, talked about his 'Jesuitical discipline', relentless drive, and total mental dedication. The profile examined de Castella's family life and his racing tactics all in the context of his single-minded determination to succeed at running. Marathon running is so physically stressful that de Castella insists on running only one or two marathons a year. Sometimes after a race his feet become a mass of blood-blisters which don't heal before he races again (30 October '82).

This emphasis on physical pain and mental endurance comes through more strongly in a *Telegraph* report on de Castella's main rival, Cuban-American Alberto Salazar. Salazar is shown photographed in training with a special face mask which simulates different altitudes. De Castella has been studying film of Salazar's win in the New York marathon to figure out his running strategy. De Castella, like all professional sportsmen, now approaches his sport scientifically. The *Telegraph* describes him as a 'sports scientist'; he is employed part-time at the Australian Institute of Sport in Canberra—the country's main sports think-tank.

A marathon man, that is, must have a scientific approach, great natural ability, and an 'intense, ice-cold deliberate commitment'. De Castella's achievements have certainly impressed and inspired others. His brilliant win in the Commonwealth Games Marathon was recognised by the ABC's award for Sportsman of the Year. Months later the *SMH* ran a human interest story about a fourteen year old girl from

Sydney's outer south-western suburbs. She had cancer in one elbow but remained dedicated to running and spoke of de Castella as her hero (28 January '83).

Temperamental Tennis Men

Professional tennis is as individualistic as long-distance running. It is an intensely psychological game. In three years on the junior tennis circuit in south-east Queensland in the late fifties, the thing most forcefully drummed into me was the need to have 'a killer instinct'. In any tennis match where two players have the same natural ability, the winner will be the one most mentally determined.

Unlike football or cricket, postwar Australian tennis was professionalised before the media incorporation of sport in the seventies. Professionalisation came first in tennis because of the influence of the American-based pro circuit; it was cheaper to fly tennis players overseas to compete than football or cricket teams. Tennis is also traditionally a more socially elite game. Physical space for tennis courts is at a premium in London, New York or Sydney. Because of its earlier professionalisation, Australian tennis has had no great players in the last ten years with the exception of women's tennis stars Court and Cawley. It is not nostalgic to say that Newcombe and Roche were pale imitations of Hoad and Rosewall. There was an idealism about tennis in the fifties and early sixties it no longer has. There was a sportsmanship and generosity displayed by men like Frank Sedgman which makes the tantrums of McEnroe and Connors seem ridiculous.

But each generation plays sport its own way. The dominance of temperamental, colourful figures like McEnroe, Vilas, Connors and Gerulaitis make up tennis's new TV image—fast, colourful, volatile and intermittently nasty. There is no body-contact in tennis, so aggression in the sport takes the form of hostile gamesmanship directed against the opponent, and—in a radical break with the past—linesmen and umpires.

TV coverage of tennis shows us the player's emotions in close up, their joy and rage. Meanwhile on the TV audio track Australian tennis commentary, except for that of some ex-players such as Neale Fraser and Ken McGregor, is often banal and inane. There are no distinguished Australian tennis commentators. American tennis commentary, like their sports talk generally, is more informed and less patronising. Lacking the capacity to talk creatively about the endless procession of

TV 'specials', the slightest points of conflict or difficulty are theatrically dramatised by tennis commentators, who begin to sound like Oz echoes of Jack Little, the expatriate American wrestling commentator of the fifties.

TV attention is awarded most to top men's events, then to women's tennis, and to the increasing number of junior matches. Each of these is presented by the media in a different emotional frame. The top men's events are represented as conflict, women's tennis is portrayed more as the triumph of dedication, while junior tennis is ambition and hope for the future.

The conflict dimension of modern tennis is clearest in press coverage of the top men stars. 'BIG STEVE: THE DAY HE NEARLY FLATTENED MCENROE', wrote the *Sun*, profiling Texan Steve Denton. Denton—'passive and gentle by nature'—had almost beaten McEnroe up in the Wimbledon changing rooms (8 December '82). Or, 'MCENROE'S RAGE JUSTIFIED', wrote Newcombe in a variant. According to Newk, McEnroe's conflict with a New York umpire was justified. Nicknamed 'the Brat' by the sports press and his opponents, McEnroe's tantrums have made him the one you love to hate. There seems to be a definite emotional release involved for sports audiences in performances like this. 'People just wanted to get involved,' complained McEnroe about the New York incident. 'Even though they had no idea what they were getting involved in. It proves they're jerks. It seems like they're just waiting for me.' This is the hothouse atmosphere of TV men's tennis today.

The outstanding Australian women's TV tennis star of the last few years has been Evonne Cawley. Women's tennis is important in sports news, as otherwise women's sports get little regular media coverage. In the Australian context as well, Cawley and Court have been great champions to compare favourably with overseas stars.

Women's tennis is less conflictual than men's. Despite a few theatrical performances, it retains more of tennis' traditional genteel qualities. Women tennis stars are still often reported as relying on their husbands or father-figures for moral support and financial guidance, where men tennis stars are more likely to be written up for their love lives. Ironically, the Women's Tennis Association is moving to block attempts to combine the Australian Men's and Women's Open events because their operation is financially viable as it stands (*S*, 6 December '82).

Evonne Cawley's unique place in Australian sporting culture is due to her being both a champion woman tennis player and an Aboriginal. In a country where national guilt over racism runs at an intermittently high level, Cawley's success has received frequent media attention. Yet some of the popular sports gossip in the press about her comes close to reproducing the old racist stereotypes. Describing her 'rollercoaster' tennis style, one *Sun* columnist wrote 'Hit a screamer of a shot here, go walkabout for a while, fluff one there, then crack such an unplayable ball that the world's best can only stand and watch it whizz past' (29 November '82). Granted, temperamental volatility can be a problem for players of any sport, but discussing this in terms of her race is patronising.

In a more serious profile of Cawley in the *National Times* she was presented as 'The Millionairess: how the quiet Evonne Goolagong became the rich and worldly Mrs Cawley' (19 December '82). This article by David Hickie explained her popularity in terms of her good nature and on-court enthusiasm, as compared to the 'twisted temperament of McEnroe, the robot-like concentration of Lendl, the agonisings of Navratilova', and so on.

But it also treated Cawley's sometimes awkward position in public as a successful Aboriginal sportswoman—the first one. She has taken legal action against *The Bulletin* for publishing a poem by Kevin Gilbert which accused her of not telling the world about the oppression of Australian blacks. Cawley also has been criticised for not supporting Billie Jean King and other breakaway women players who fought successfully for equal prize money in the early seventies. At the same time, this profile of Cawley emphasised her no-nonsense attitude to the game and simple enthusiasm for life. Her normality is favourably contrasted with the lifestyles of Billie Jean King and Navratilova and the cloistered existences of young teenage stars like Tracy Austin. The role of her husband, Robert Cawley, is routinely mentioned, as is the support she gets from surrogate father-figure Teddy Tinling. Cawley's Australian media image locates and isolates her as a black island of normality in a white sea of temperamentally selfish behaviour.

Junior tennis is at the bottom of the TV ratings pile. Australia has no outstanding junior tennis players in international teams, but the search goes on. Melbourne seventeen-year-old Pat Cash is currently the most visible junior tennis star. Unfortunately, the professionals tell us, Australia has no great junior tennis training programs as in the U.S.A. Ex-players—now promoters—Newcombe and Roche, however, have committed themselves to national tennis training schemes. This trend is linked with the expansion of sports-based faculties in Australian tertiary education. What was once 'PE' in the curriculum is now 'Human Movement Studies'. Academically inclined sportsmen collect American PhDs in the subject, come back to Australia, write sports sociology, build education sports programmes, and move into administrative positions in state health departments.

Football Violence

Violence in long-distance running is self-directed, whereas in tennis it's expressed more in ruthless player rivalries and displays of temper. In professional football physical aggression is a routine part of the game. Evening and Sunday papers covering Sydney League and Union games regularly carry banners like: 'PARRA, SAINTS AT WAR!: They hit us with head-butts, stiff arms, promoters' punches and kicks' (*M*, 21 June '82). 'ROOS BRAWL: But they're still the greatest' (*S*, 29 November '82).

The provincial press presents a less sensational account of football and sometimes openly criticises violence in the game. The Armidale paper, *The Northern Daily Leader*, for instance, reports on the city as a regional football capital, linking it with sports programmes at the University of New England (14 January '83). In 1981 the *Illawarra Daily Mercury* carried a front page editorial censuring League violence in the wake of a bloody Wollongong Steeler's match. Football violence is also sometimes given as the reason for coaches' resignations. After Jack Gibson quit as president of the N.S.W. Rugby League Players Association he said: 'I feel uncomfortable with certain things in the game ... I don't have any respect for players who bite ... the coaches are to blame but I can't excuse the players.'

As the football season draws on, lists of injured players mount up. Preoccupation with health and injuries become a constant preoccupation of the media. Players themselves are well aware of the risks. Wayne Pearce, a member of the victorious 'Roo tour of England, wrote for the *Mirror* predicting that the lifespan of League players would rapidly become shorter. New rules make the game faster and more physically demanding, and the age range of players is getting progressively younger (2 February '83).

Pressure on players is not only physical, but financial. The sports press regularly carries stories about players who have missed out on the big money and their career problems. With the financial system now governing Sydney teams and clubs there's little room for sentiment in dealing with players. According to Easts coach Laurie Freier, spiralling player payments are killing club loyalties—two of Easts best players had just been bought by Manly (*S*, 31 December '82). Canterbury player Peter Casilles also got short shrift from his club after playing 192 first grade games for them. Casilles had wanted to make it an even 200 but found himself relegated to third grade because of new player acquisitions by his club (*S*, 6 December '82). Again, Geoff Robinson had to return to Canberbury because he'd gone broke after signing a three year $90 000 contract. 'I can play football till I'm thirty,' he said. 'But I have to hold a job till I'm sixty.'

More employees are knocking back footballers as workers because of time lost through training and injuries (*M*, 2 February '83). In reaction to these pressures, and the financial collapse of clubs like Newtown, some League players have attempted to introduce an element of player-power in organising the financial side of the game, as at Cronulla (*S*, 21 January '83).

Footballers rarely get detailed personal profiles in the way sportsmen in tennis or cricket do. There is also a fair amount of media abuse and petty sniping levelled at footballers when they aren't being eulogised. Mike Gibson slated the 'ROOS CLEAN SWEEP BRITISH TOUR' in *The Bulletin*, claiming their standards weren't up to the 'Roos of '63. 'They're a great side,' he said. 'But not the greatest.' (*B*, 7 December '82). Similarly, *Sun* columnist Richard Sleeman tipped a bucket on the legendary Ray Price. Price had criticised journalists for 'waiting around like vultures' at the 'Roos' Leeds hotel for something to go wrong (*S*, 6 December '82). League had enough troubles already, Sleeman claimed, compared with the image of sophistication and good taste of VFL in Sydney.

Cricket Men

While football is regionally and socially divided in Australia, and tennis is individualistic, cricket is still the most truly national Australian game. The media constantly use cricket as a means of locating Australia's place in the world. Where football replaced baseball as the top U.S. media sport after World War II, cricket is still holding on to its premier position in Australian sporting culture.

The cricketing world is made up of Commonwealth countries— England, Australia, New Zealand, West Indies, India, Pakistan, Sri Lanka—and the now-excluded South Africa. Within this wider setting of old-fashioned imperial nationalism, commercial pressures on cricket have re-shaped the game for the media. One-day cricket, coloured uniforms, and visor-like face-guards for batsmen all make 1980s cricket more speedy, colourful and marketable. Declining real cricket attendances are balanced by administrators against their sport's TV appeal. Direct aggression in cricket is expressed at a range of different levels, from spectator riots to bodyline bowling. Yet cricket is more like tennis in its uses of conflict because it's not a body-contact sport. As with tennis, it gives more prominence to individual performance, but in a team context.

But police and players have been injured by spectator invasions of the pitch in recent Test incidents at Perth. In December '82 the *Sun* carried a report 'TOP POLICE SQUAD TO STOP SCG "VIOLENCE"'. This reported crowd control procedures by members of armed police, including the 1984-ish Tactical Response Group, in taking preventive measures at the SCG, like the establishment of a two metre wide 'no-go' area (30 December '82). Real aggression in the game, however, comes out more in the confrontations between players and sometimes players and umpires.

Lillee has been the brightest firebrand in contemporary Australian cricket. He still attracts heavy media coverage. Excerpts from his most recent autobiography were serialised in the Sydney evening press in mid-'82 with the banner: 'WHY I BLEW UP OVER THAT TIN BAT' (*M*, 20 August '82). Six months later the *Mirror* re-told exactly the same story from Greg Chappell's viewpoint. An accompanying photo of Lillee was titled: 'POWER: the daunting view as Dennis Lillee thunders in for the kill' (27 January '83). In his first autobiography (1976) Lillee described his intimidatory tactics:

> Batsmen are like thieves to me, desperately trying to steal from me the ascendancy I believe is mine. And I treat them like faceless thieves ... I try to find something about the faceless batsman that really annoys me then I build on that until it becomes a sort of hatred that burns in my guts until I get them out ... not many batsmen recover from a really good bouncer. (Atyeo, 295)

Lillee and Greg Chappell currently occupy the same page in the *Mirror* as featured sports-writers, but cricket players don't necessarily make good journalists. The Lillee–Chappell style of sports journalism is often dull and sometimes sounds like a mutual admiration society. 'The Chappells will do me ... against all kinds of bowling,' Lillee recently wrote in his column, while on the same page Chappell was advocating Lillee's return to Test bowling (16 January '82). Players are taking over a larger share of sports journalism in Australia and overseas. 'Fiery England all-rounder' Ian Botham writes a column in the London *Sun*, where he recently blasted the low standard of Australian umpires for England's Ashes defeat (*S*, 9 January '83). This way partisanship on the field is transferred directly to the sporting press.

Again, the main pressures on cricket are generated by corporate sponsorship and the media. Money is the real centre-piece of the game and this is taken for granted. A rumoured $250 000 offer to South Australian cricketer David Hookes to captain Victoria was a recent page-one *Mirror* story (27 January '83). The pressures from sponsorship and one-day cricket and other media-inspired rule changes boost cricket partisanship between and within teams. None of the top cricketers are free from media criticism. A *Sunday Telegraph* columnist recently claimed that Kim Hughes had been set up by Greg Chappell, so that Chappell would return triumphant after Hughes' disasters (30 January '83).

Australian cricket also has come under more direct political pressure than other sports because of the international arguments about the place of South Africa in world contests. In January '83 Malcolm Fraser banned West Indian cricketers who had taken part in the rebel tour of South Africa. Other ban-breaking tours to South Africa in 1982 by English and Sri Lankan teams had already led to bans by their own national cricket authorities.

Since its exile from international cricket in 1970, South African officials have intermittently, with some recent success, tried to break the bans. One *Sun* article on the issue predicted that Lillee and other leading Oz cricket stars would soon receive South African offers they'd find difficult to refuse. The only long-term effective counter measure would be for more sponsorship deals in non-South African countries to keep players home (3 February '83).

Sportsmen, Violence and the Media

Sport in most industrial societies is commercially based, conflict oriented, and is used as a symbol of chauvinistic nationalism. More specifically, Australian sportsmen are caught between the pressures of media incorporation, commercial sponsorship by alcohol and tobacco companies, and politically motivated state and federal health policies. The overall picture of sport presented by the media reproduces competitive, individualistic and commercial values which reinforce the same values in work and public life. Sport is cynically used by politicians, the media, and big business to promote patriotism, moral authority, and to make profits. Violence and conflict in sports comes out at three main levels—in the game itself, in exaggerated media versions, and through the governmental and corporate use of sport to advertise health, nationalism, the media itself, alcohol and tobacco, and political parties as in Liberal TV advertising in the '83 election.

Channel 10's President of Sport, Brian Morris, commented on 10's acquisition of Australian TV rights to the 1984 Los Angeles Olympic Games that his company's aim was to dominate sports TV in Australia. These would be the first free enterprise games in history, he said: 'The Disney organisation has been hired to structure the opening and closing ceremonies. There might never be games like this again'. He also acknowledged that the new trend in TV was for networks to create their own sports events, rather than rely on traditional ones. Concerning new sports, the Channel's aim was to select those with TV potential and invest in them on a long-term basis. The Ten Network already has broadcast FIFA World Youth Soccer internationally to a world audience of 750 million (*T*, 12 September '82).

Companies most heavily involved in sports sponsorship are Benson and Hedges in cricket, Marlboro in tennis, and all major Australian liquor companies in football. Three of the current trustees of the prestigious SCG—Sir Nicholas Shehadie, Alan Davidson, and Marlene Matthews—are associated with Rothmans, though the Rothmans National Sports Foundation is not involved in any sponsorship of sport at the SCG (*SMH*, 15 January '83).

Nor does it have to be. The informal associations between business and sports sponsorship are well-established in Australian public life. The 1983 'Battle of the Codes' in Melbourne was introduced on Channel 7 by the Victorian Minister for Youth, Sport, and Recreation, Neil Tresizes. Mr Tresizes made his opening speech—'mumble, mumble, good deal of idle time for so many young people, encourage them to play sport'—in front of a huge Carlton United Breweries outdoor advertisement (5 February '83). The same week, N.S.W. Minister for Leisure, Sport, and Tourism, Michael Cleary, was proudly announcing the introduction of League TAB cards and Michael Edgley's promotion of the Harold Park trots (*Bondi Spectator*, 27 January '83).

The number and variety of sporting activities in Australia are so great that sports commentators have no trouble in finding subject matter. There is a constant stream of sports talk on Australian radio and TV which saturates the weekend and recurs mid-week. Commentators like Frank Hyde and Ron Casey (League), Alan McGilvray and Norman May (cricket), and Bill Collins and Des Hoysted (racing), are as well known as many sports stars. The older style of low-key gentlemanly commentary is still practiced by the ABC—though some Commonwealth Games commentators were hysterically nationalistic—but younger commercial sports commentators can be rabidly partisan and opinionated.

Commercial sports journalists and broadcasters often have sports backgrounds in one area, but the trend towards continuous sports-talk means that they have to talk about other sports of which they have no personal experience. The result of this, and of the complexities involved in talking at all seriously about sport, is a series of fabrications and fantasies about sport and society. In these discussions the media's role is rarely examined.

Saturday afternoon radio sports talk shows are the best examples. In 2GB's Saturday morning sports show headed by Richard Fiske an angry call came in from one listener complaining about comments on soccer by Peter Peters. Peters had disparaged the Australian Youth Soccer team coach as 'an out-of-work Pommie'. The caller spoke with an ethnic accent and, to bolster his argument with Peters, pointed out that he wasn't English himself. Peters response was sarcastic: 'I know you're not. That's a great revelation.'

Later in the morning another caller wanted to know why Rex Mossop, Channel 7's Director of Sports, was calling soccer games, as Mossop's background was League. Fiske gave an unusually straight answer—that Channel 7 was 'trying to create more of an ocker Australian image and less of an ethnic image for soccer' (5 February '83).

In the afternoon another 2GB sportsman, Kerry O'Keefe, rudely criticised women callers for asking stupid questions. He copped a lot of flack for this from men and women callers, but defended himself in these terms: 'Isn't it great discussing the merits of cricket with a thirty-five-year-old housewife. Is this how I'm supposed to spend the rest of my days?' Listener criticism was defused next by a serious discussion about whether Kim Hughes was real captain-of-Australia material. In a metaphorical and political sense, most Australian media arguments about sport boil down to arguments about who's going to be captain.

When ex-Australian journalist Don Atyeo published a timely book about sports violence in 1979 it went down like a lead balloon in Australia. Sport is one of the most touchy of subjects for Australians. Criticism of sportsmen is often taken to be criticism of everything Australian. Atyeo's conclusion was that sports violence does not reduce violence in society, but adds to it. The commercial media's treatment of Australian sport reproduces a code of aggressive masculine interpersonal values which preach the virtues of being individualistic, aggressive and competitive.

5 Men and Anti-Gay Repression

There is little tradition of speaking freely about homosexuality in Australia. Dennis Altman stands out as the first established and explicitly gay social critic, but much of what is published about gay life is buried in government reports. Public discussion also has focused exclusively on homosexual men. It leaves lesbian women to one side, and assumes that homosexual issues have no relevance to heterosexual men. I am interested in precisely this last issue—the cultural influence of gay life on heterosexual men.

While homosexual behaviour is as old as society itself, gay consciousness is a post-sixties development. There is now a positive connotation in describing someone as 'gay', where 'homosexual' is a word some people still use negatively to convey associations of criminality and depravity.

Though mainstream Oz culture traditionally has rejected gay experience, it now is moving towards its co-option and tacit acceptance. I want to bring out four sides to this—the rejection of and discrimination against gays, heterosexual fear and ignorance about homosexuality, the commercial and media co-option and inversion of gay life, and last its qualified acceptance.

Rejection, Violence and Discrimination

Andrea, a now-retired society journalist and Sydney radio personality wrote in 1975: 'I still meet people who are outraged by the mere idea of homosexuals. Australia must be the last bastion of a masculinity so strident that it professes utter revulsion at homosexuality.'

Why do Australian men sometimes react against gay men so violently? Perhaps because homosexuality was historically an import from Britain in the first place. There was a submerged tradition of homosexual aestheticism in English high culture, with members of the clergy, diplomats, writers and artists who were homosexual. Some of the early penal administrators also added to a brutally anti-homosexual climate. English colonists like Samuel Marsden and William Logan took sado-masochistic pleasure in ordering prisoners to be flogged. If some of the first Australian homosexuals were English and of a higher social class, that was two reasons for the 'currency lads' to hate them.

Some groups which actively oppose homosexual law reform today have issued literature which supports violence. Through 1977-9 pro- and anti-gay groups fought about the distribution of a Festival of Light pamphlet written by a woman barrister. This argued that homosexual soliciting by a man should be accepted by the courts as legitimate defence against a murder charge. Gay Rights responded that the FOL was condoning anti-homosexual murder.

Anti-homosexual violence is nothing new in Australia. The practice of 'poofter bashing' was one of the marks of manhood for tough young men. There were ten murders of homosexual men between 1970 and 1975 nationally, and in mid-1980 the *Sydney Star*, a weekly give-away gay paper, claimed a new wave of anti-gay violence was developing. In October 1981 the 'gay blade' killings took place in Sydney's eastern suburbs, sensationally involving the murder of the Greek Consul-General. Sydney gay magazines still carry warnings to their readers about parks which are being prowled by violently anti-homosexual men.

Yet avoidance and discrimination are types of social and psychological violence practiced in everyday life which constitute the most demoralising interpersonal experiences for gay men. Discrimination is the practical form that violent prejudice takes in daily life. I want to present two unpleasant examples here, one from the 1982 Anti-Discrimination Board Report on homosexuality, and one from personal knowledge.

The first case concerns a 'Mr A', who in 1978 was pressured into resigning from his job as a senior officer in a church social welfare department. After Mr A had publicly supported the Royal Commission on Human Relationships recommendations about underprivileged children and homosexuals, he had been subjected to telephone death threats and abusive mail. Next a campaign for his dismissal was launched by a small minority of his junior colleagues. That failed, but he was pressured into resigning on other grounds. He was re-employed in a similar job by another church welfare agency, but was yet again discriminated against and forced to resign (ADB, 490).

The second case was told to me in 1977 by a friend then employed at a workers' health centre in Sydney's Western suburbs. A middle-aged man had approached him for medical care and personal counselling. 'George' was a factory worker, married, with teenage children. George had been unhappily homosexual for years. He lacked the social resources to understand his own position, and considered his homosexuality an illness. He conducted his sex-life furtively in parks and public lavatories in constant fear of police detection. When his wife and children discovered George's homosexuality they humiliated him, even making him do the dishes dressed in women's clothes. Popular views of homosexuality often link it with effeminism and women's roles like this.

These cases suggest that if middle- and working-class discrimination against homosexuals is equally vicious, working-class discrimination may be mainly ignorant, where middle-class prejudice is more vindictive. Mr A at least had the personal resources to have accepted his own sexuality. His 'problem' occurred because his homosexuality became public knowledge. George, however, lacked the resources to understand that part of his own life. As horrible as the reaction of his wife and kids was, at least it seems to have come from a spontaneous sense of anger and shock.

Heterosexual Men's Fear and Ignorance

Australian men have a gut-level negative emotional reaction to homosexual men. The problem is mainly an emotional one for men to bring themselves to look at the issues in the first place, not an intellectual difficulty in coping with the subject. The basis of this negativism is ignorance—both plain and wilful ignorance. As the Royal Commission on Human Relationships said: 'At the moment people are afraid because they are ignorant. Education has not helped them to see that their own basic life patterns will not be adversely affected' (by homosexual law reform) (*HR*, 4/113).

A repressed factor in men's avoidance of homosexuals is their fear that their own homosexual desire may be aroused. Human sexual behaviour is a continuum along which homosexuality and heterosexuality are overlapping forms of behaviour. Biologically and practically, homosexuality is a normal if minority experience; culturally, however, homosexuality has been tabooed until recently.

Men are more likely to become homosexual than women, and homosexual experimentation is not unusual for many men who later become heterosexual. Llewellyn-Jones has estimated that in 1981 there were three million homosexual men in the U.S., one million in Britain, and more than 300 000 in Australia. One in every 25 men in those countries is likely to have a homosexual orientation. Because of these links between homosexuality and the 'normal' development of masculinity, the fear of homosexuality for some men is like the danger of Narcissus' image shattering in the water—one morning you may wake up and find yourself homosexual.

So while men need to unite with women, they need to reject homosexuals publicly as a way of coping with their fear of social rejection by other men if they fail to do so. Men are expected to be tough, and being a tough Australian man still means being anti-gay.

Some National Party politicians, for example, are pretty tough and ignorant. N.S.W. MLA Jim Brown recently claimed that:

> I do not expect people to be bashed because they engage in this shocking practice [homosexuality] ... but if teachers were to encourage ... young boys to be manly and take part in proper sports, then perhaps the reason for the bashing would be removed. (*Campaign*, December '82)

As prejudiced and as ignorant as such views are, they express one of the common-sense views about homosexuals—that they are not 'manly'.

I want to argue that it is not homosexuality, but aggressive masculinity, which is a social problem. David Fernbach, an American gay writer, sees homosexuals as effeminate as well, but in a positive way. Fernbach argues that boys who grow up homosexual continue to identify more with their mothers than their fathers. Heterosexual boys break this initial strong maternal identification early in their lives, and masculinity is reinforced for them later in sports, peer groups, and at school. In this sense, Fernbach sees gay men as effeminate:

> Pejorative and inadequate as this word evidently is, it has a solid core of truth in implying that we have failed to complete the course of masculinisation, having dropped out a significant way before the end of the process, and thus retain part of that feminity which masculinisation is designed to repress. (Fernbach, 92)

Fernbach's version of Freud adds an explicitly political factor to the social construction of homosexuality. Because gay men are basically effeminate, he argues, they contradict the norms of the gender system. Where the expression of homosexuality as a normal male developmental experience does not contradict society's gender system, the public proclamation of gay identity does. It contradicts conventional masculinity because it both excludes women as social sexual partners, and incorporates many levels of feminine culture. Women are criticised for narcissism and vanity, just as gays are. The connection is most explicit in male porn fantasies about lesbian sex.

So we return to the common-sense view of Mr Brown that homosexuals are like women. It makes sense: chauvinist men dislike gays because they see them as being like women. What really is at issue is why men should dislike women in the first place. Men who are anti-gay will also be anti-female.

Men who fear homosexuality in themselves project their own antisocial fantasies onto society while claiming homosexuals are to blame. The conventional fears about homosexuals—that they will influence younger men or children to become gay, pass on sexual diseases, molest male children, and destroy family life—can all be interpreted as extensions of heterosexual men's own anti-social attitudes.

The issue of child molestation is most clearly linked with the projection of heterosexual men's own anti-social attitudes. The Anti-Discrimination Board's research showed that agencies concerned with child sexual abuse felt the main problem was that of adult men molesting girls, especially in family situations. Statistics about child abuse in N.S.W. establish that it is much more a heterosexual problem. Also, some studies showed that the majority of men who sexually assaulted young boys considered themselves heterosexual (ADB, 176).

This is not to deny that there are cases where homosexual men have seduced boys. In 1979 Clarence Osborne, a middle-aged court reporter in Brisbane, suicided after police had found out about his long history of sexual activity with boys. Paul Wilson's study of the Osborne case shows a man who was considered an otherwise respectable, if socially isolated, man. He also never used force in his encounters. Contrary to the media sensationalism about Osborne, he had been an ordinary man whose staggering success in seducing boys had depended mainly on him being a sympathetic older man who was ready to listen. Some of the boys involved had expressed regret at Osborne's death, and explicitly rejected media treatment of him as a 'monster'.

The most depressing feature which emerges from the Osborne story is the extent to which so many of the young men concerned were alienated from their families before they met him. They had come from a wide range of social backgrounds in Brisbane, but most couldn't communicate with their family members on an open emotional basis. Many of the boys treated Osborne as a surrogate father or uncle. In return he gave them a warmth and understanding they apparently couldn't get from their own fathers.

Commercial and Media Co-option

Commercial co-option is the normal way alternative lifestyles are dealt with by capitalism. Yesterday's radical slogans are cynically recycled as today's advertising jingles. It happened to feminism, and now there are signs that gay people—especially gay men—are also fast being incorporated into the mould of conservative consumerism.

Social life in Sydney's gay scene rests fairly securely on a commercial base in the first place. Oxford Street, the city's main gay area, is full of discos, pubs, and coffee shops catering for the gay market. The largest Australian gay magazine, *Campaign*, is commercially oriented, and the Gay Business Association enters floats in the annual Gay Mardi Gras. The Mardi Gras had originally been conceived as the movement's political event but has been co-opted by more conservative commercial interests.

A recent example of commercial co-option was the decision of Ansett airlines to advertise in *Campaign*. A November '82 press release by Ansett acknowledged that the Australian gay community had been ignored by the public, but now that was changing. 'Ansett has stressed however,' the release went, 'that it is offering no more to the gay community than it is already offering to minority ethnic groups or indeed to any of its existing travellers.' Ansett wants gay dollars, but doesn't want to be specially identified with the gay scene.

Advertising tends to set the pace in the media's co-option of gay life and the rest of the media follows on. Some gay characters, for instance, now have been presented in a reasonably positive way in films like *Starstruck* and *Lonely Hearts*. A new concentration on the homoerotic potential of the male body is more visible in TV advertising, notably for underclothes. Similarly, a few of Frank Moorhouse's stories have presented homosexual characters in some depth.

There is, however, a double standard in the commercial media's treatment of gay culture. The ADB report found there was a general lack of coverage of gay issues, alternating with negative sensationalism about events like the 1978 Gay Rights demonstration. Until the late sixties, news about homosexuality was drawn almost exclusively from overseas sources, mostly involving prominent men in the U.K. involved in spy scandals.

Gay media reform groups have become increasingly organised in monitoring negative media treatment. They made critical submissions about TV coverage in 1979 and 1982 to hearings by the Australian Broadcasting Tribunal, and have criticised treatment of educational news in the Sydney press. When the *St George and Sutherland Shire Leader* ran a headline in 1979 'NO QUEER SEX FOR STUDENTS', about sex education in the schools, complaints by gay activists eventually led to the censure of the paper by the Australian Press Council (ADB, 241).

Another recurrent concern gays have with media treatment of their lives is that they should not be publicly identified if they don't wish to be. This was a major issue in the wake of the 1978 demonstrations and arrests, when the *Sydney Morning Herald* printed long lists of names of people arrested. Subsequently the Press Council rejected gay complaints about this procedure—and the Fairfax group is not a member of the Council in the first place. So it is not just by stereotyping or ignoring homosexuals as a group that the media threatens gays, but also by its public identification of some homosexuals who then may lose their jobs if they are teachers, or employed in other vulnerable roles.

Overall, the commercial media reflect and reinforce public ignorance and indifference to gay life-styles. They do this by avoidance, selective reporting, and stereotyping. Periodically the print media, notably the *Australian* and the *National Times*, run sympathetic articles to cash in on the gay commercial market.

The broadcast media, on the other hand, traditionally rely on entertainment, variety shows and films—areas in which gays have often been employed. Especially in the presentation of entertainment and comedy, a hybrid style has been developed by a number of successful Australian TV personalities which is latently camp. This combination of avoidance and commercial acceptance in the print media, and continued negative stereotyping and mock imitation in TV entertainment, inverts normal public standards about men's behaviour.

Radio and TV are more likely than the press to make outright fun of homosexuals or use them as part of the entertainment. Singleton on 2KY still often refers to them as 'poofs', while John Laws on 2UE used an Anzac Day confrontation between gay activities and the Victorian RSL in 1982 as a funny introduction to his morning show (*ST*, 25 April '82). More seriously, the popular press uses homosexuality in prisons as a sign of the evils of prison life. When a Queensland MP reported to parliament that some warders in a Brisbane jail were homosexual, this made front page news in the Melbourne *Truth* (15 January '83).

The symbolic inversion of gay culture in the commercial media leads to some bizarre results. One is the enormous emphasis on images of tough men in body-contact situations in TV ads. Commercials for alcohol, especially, have promoted beer sales by associating drinking with images of tough footballers. These ads dwell on scenes of violent conflict on the field, followed by the reaffirmation of cameraderie in the dressing room, with male nudity in the showers, and rough friendly body contact.

I am not implying that Australian footballers are repressed homosexuals in real life. Homoerotic behaviour positively avoids and discourages explicit sexual contact between men. It has to. From the convicts, the explorers, the miners and bush workers, the soldiers posted overseas, through to men working in isolated environments today and prisoners in jails, homosexuality in Australia in those settings has been something inflicted on men by force of circumstance, instead of a free choice. What is puzzling, though, is the emphasis on male body contact highlighted by advertising.

Another example of manipulative media handling of male sexuality is the growth of elements of S/M (sado-masochism) in media imagery about heterosexual life. Examples of this range from the taken-for-granted sexual sadism in the James Bond films (the original spy films, like Hitchcock's *Secret Agent*, featured gay characters as baddies), to the foregrounding of S/M styles in high fashion trends and TV advertising using punk and leather imagery, even for sweets!

Media attention to S/M peaked in Australia in 1980 with the release of the controversial and violent film *Cruising*. This concerned a policeman's hunt for a sadistic killer of homosexual men in New York's Christopher Street. Though supposedly based on a true story, national gay organisations in the U.S., the U.K., and Australia censured the film and picketed screenings on the grounds that it equated homosexuality with violence and sado-masochism.

Al Pacino, who starred in the film, previously had played a gay bank robber in *Dog Day Afternoon*. At the end of *Cruising*, having survived New York's sleaziest gay bars and clubs, and having caught and stabbed the killer, Pacino stands alone before his bathroom mirror. He looks worriedly at his face, while in the next room his girl-friend is trying on his leather clothes. This ambiguous ending can be read conventionally to mean that Pacino is verifying he still looks like a real man; it can be read conservatively in terms of the implied relationships between the homosexual and the criminal; or it can be taken radically, as a statement about the presence of sado-masochism in 'normal' heterosexual relationships.

The process of commercial co-option of gay culture is most advanced in the U.S., which remains a strong direct influence on the Sydney gay scene. Even Hollywood, with recent films like *Making Love*, now has moved slightly towards a favourable presentation of gay life. However, as Paul Foss argued in a review of this film and *Taxi Zum Klo* (a totally different, irreverent and bawdy German gay film), current films about gays seem to be preoccupied with the good management of gay relationships (*Gay Information*, November '82). In other words, the heterosexual couple remains the desirable role model for gays as well.

This reduces homosexual lifestyles to carbon copies of conventional heterosexuality.

Qualified Acceptance

Perhaps the strongest cultural factor which will eventually achieve greater acceptance for gay lifestyles in Australia is the increased openness and experimentation in heterosexual experiences over the last decade. Even family oriented magazines like *Good Housekeeping* are now running articles which discuss how some marriages and relationships work better when the partners don't live together.

The most directly relevant influence here is the development of bisexuality as a socially acceptable option. The sixties counter-culture was originally associated with elements of bisexual behaviour and role reversal in fashion and style, but hippie men still seemed to go along dreamily with the Mother Earth idea of women looking after babies and growing organic vegetables. Then in the mid-seventies a stronger American emphasis on fashionable bisexuality began to reach Australia.

Californian self-realisation philosophies usually emphasised the 'normality' of bisexual behaviour, and this greater tolerance was also advocated by the Australian adult sex education magazine *Forum*. Another important overseas influence, if less idealistic, was the semi-public declaration of bisexuality (and, less often, homosexuality) by leading American and British pop stars including David Bowie, Marc Bolan, Bette Midler and Elton John. There have been few direct Australian counter-parts, but pop-stars like Red Symons, Richard Clapton and Mick Conway have at times projected sexually ambiguous images. Now the trend has been taken further by more bizarre overseas stars like Boy George of Culture Club or Grace Jones, who has a sharp s/M image.

In terms of law reform, legislation to change the existing anti-homosexual laws now has been introduced in N.S.W., after the decriminalisation acts passed in South Australia, the A.C.T., and Victoria. Yet it seems by no means certain that this reform will succeed in the near future.

Australian society is still sharply divided about homosexuality. A minority of people actively oppose law reform, but they are especially outspoken and actively linked with right-wing religious pressure groups, led by fundamentalist Christians like Fred Nile. National opinion polls in 1973, 1974, 1976 and 1978 indicated a fairly wide level of public support for the legalisation of homosexuality, but some of these results were equivocal. The 1982 ADB Report concluded that apart from one earlier 1967 survey, all later polls had shown a majority of people more or less favourably disposed to such changes (ADB, 233).

Current Australian attitudes to homosexuality seem to be becoming more accepting, but this acceptance is highly qualified. The 1977 Royal Commission on Human Relationships drew attention to this by referring to two levels of public feelings towards homosexuals. At the superficial level, 'most people wanted to see homosexuals with the same rights and responsibilities as heterosexuals', but at a deeper level was the proviso 'so long as they keep away from us and our children.' (HR, 5/113).

There are a lot of positive things Australian men could learn from gay men if they were willing. There is a greater sensitivity to interpersonal relations, and a greater willingness to be emotionally open, among many gay people—homosexual men and lesbians. Some lesbian parents are extremely concerned and caring parents. Yet while a number of Australia's leading writers, artists and entertainers are gay, even their stature has not given them the confidence to acknowledge their sexuality publicly.

I don't mean to idealise gay life naively. It has its own particular difficulties and miseries, as brought out in films like *Nighthawks*, an English gay film. Despite this, the exaggerated hostility and fear many Australian men still seem to have about homosexuality are more unintentional expressions of the insecurity of their own masculine identities. Homosexual repression reinforces the emotional self-repression of heterosexual men.

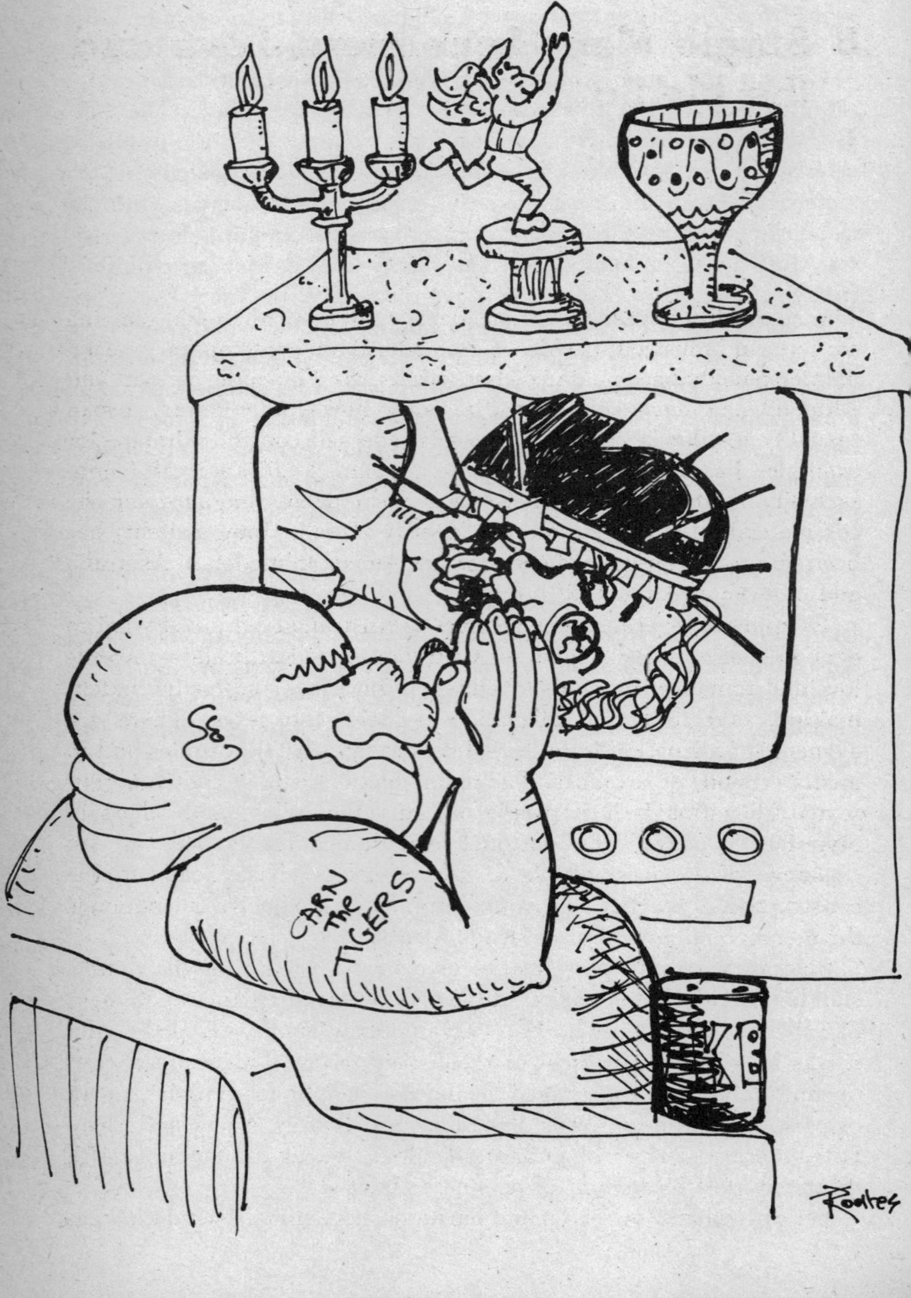
CARN the TIGERS
Rodkes

CHANNEL 2

6 Single Men—Loneliness, Love and the Media

The cultural definition of sexual identity is one of the main ongoing concerns of industrial societies. Comments about contemporary sexual politics quickly become dated, but writers like Foucault, Sennett and Altman each have emphasised recently how contemporary urban sexuality is a key means of both social and self control. Altman, for example, has argued that the recent commercialisation of homosexuality in the U.S. has acted as a fashionable vanguard for the commercialisation of heterosexual identity as well. Homosexuality has been internationalised on a commercial, American model, in Australia and elsewhere (Altman, 79).

To apply these critical perspectives to Australian culture, I want to deal with three sides of modern Australian sexual attitudes—towards love and romance, to men's loneliness in big cities and media matchmaking, and to sexual alienation between the sexes. There are elements of alienation in both real Australian sexual attitudes and in media versions of sexuality. The main characteristic of contemporary sexual alienation is how people objectify themselves and others in materialistic ways. Interpersonal communication is seen as an exchange of services, which in its anti-social phases leads to the construction of identity as a commodity. More succinctly, alienation is the commercial co-option of sexual identity.

Australian culture now has its own media version of the double standard in talking about sex. In the previous century Australian men, like their English cousins, didn't talk publicly about sex. If they did it was in scientific, medical or theological terms. This repression of openness about sex encouraged the development of a rich undergrowth of porn and smut. In 1980s Australia, post-Kinsey, Greer and Shere Hite, there is a river of public talk about sex in the media, and a genuinely greater amount of openness about sex.

Yet Australian wowserism and puritanism are still alive and kicking.

They remain strong in the churches, the schools, in councils, and many community groups. Australians are not at the end of a period of sexual liberation: they are right in the middle of it. When Sydney's first legal nude beaches opened in the mid-seventies bitter opposition came from some nearby residents. TV personality Rex Mossop actually made a citizen's arrest on one nude bather. At a more serious level, the problem has re-emerged in terms of Darlinghurst residents' opposition to street prostitution.

The media constantly treat sex as a subject of public discussion. They exploit sex commercially in advertising, regularly promote sexist stereotypes in entertainment programmes, and use sex to make hidden comments about social issues in current affairs shows. In media versions of the double standard it's now socially desirable to talk about sex—in TV advertising it seems obligatory. But sex is presented as either something to treat casually, as if all the problems have been solved, or melodramatically as if Sodom is about to appear in Sydney, Brisbane or Albury.

The commercial media frame public discussions of Australian sexuality in predictable, conventional, and materialistic categories of experience. Far more is involved than just the issues of media stereotyping of women. The whole range of emotional concerns between the sexes are organised by the media in a restricted way that emphasises the superficial, sensational and commercial in stories about sex. Sex, love and romance are staple items in the media's treatment of sexuality, yet coverage is usually about sex instead of sexuality. On the other hand, the media's attention to loneliness, alienation, rape, or domestic violence, is not given sustained attention.

Love is the Drug

Love is one of the most widely discussed and sought after experiences in the Western world. Love can be defined negatively by saying that it's a refuge from loneliness. More positively, it's a sharing of intimacy, trust and understanding—plus sex. Some Australians love God, and in some cultures people love nature. Western industrial cultures, however, highlight love of country and heterosexual romantic love, and Australians do as well.

Australian men have culturally tough and innocent sexual attitudes to women. Of course there are positive dimensions to Australian men's sexuality as well, but here I want to foreground the repressed, anti-social sides of everyday sexual attitudes and behaviour. Any statement of psychological themes of this kind only makes sense in its own cultural context. This ambivalence between toughness and innocence in men's attitudes is experienced individually, but it is partly a reflection of the influence of older Australian men's attitudes where they see their wives as possessions or partners.

More formally, Australian men's attitudes to women are regulated negatively through the alternation of a romantic and a direct set of sexual attitudes. These are psychologically convertible: they reinforce each other, and in times of personal stress or crisis, they can rapidly switch from one to the other. In terms of transactional analysis, Australian men tend to hold parental (direct) or child-like (romantic) attitudes to women.

This doesn't leave much cultural room for the development of positively realistic attitudes to relationships. Australian men are too inclined to evaluate relationships in materialistic or sentimental terms, and to have fairly low levels of expectations. Commercial media romanticism is very strong, but real Australian attitudes to love and romance are often bluntly straightforward, and prone to lapse into cynicism or pessimism.

To develop this theme I want to consider some of the different cultural levels of romanticism expressed in the media. The media treat romance both very superficially and very seriously. Escapist romanticism about love and sex is the dominant commercial model, but traditional romanticism about family ties is also central.

Vulgar romanticism is mostly about decaffeinated love, i.e. lurv. Mass advertising, especially TV ads, heavily uses vulgar romanticism as a psychological appeal. The pre-Xmas period is always overloaded with advertising messages of good cheer that tell people what they should be like. 'Over the years,' Maureen Duvall from DJ's says sagely, 'many things happen. You grow up, you get married, you have a family.' There is an unintended element of truth in trite ad spiels like this. She is rightly implying that for many of us nothing extraordinary happens. Or rather, that we best realise our identity through being breadwinners, happy family members, and proud consumers.

The latest Macdonald's commercial also sings a jolly Xmas song about sharing the good things of life, mostly between pretty, young, healthy and glamorous young couples. Love is sharing, says Macdonalds. And what is shared? Romance and french fries, says Macdonalds. Again Australians are being told that love and relationships can be defined in terms of possession, ownership, and exchange.

Naive romanticism is more about romance. It comes through most strongly in cultural productions like the English Mills and Boon novelettes for women. The popularity of Mills and Boon in Australia has been second only to the *Women's Weekly*'s. Book departments of chain stores like Coles still feature Mills and Boon prominently in their displays. One feminist study of the social values expressed in the series indicates the stereotyped way men—as well as women—are presented by Mills and Boon. Here is a typical M&B hero:

> A man in his early forties who looked younger, broad and thick set, with very black hair which was only slightly tinged with grey. His face was strong, rather than handsome, with deep-set green eyes, and a full almost sensual mouth. (Anderson, 16)

Where the hero is indomitable, the other male characters are capable of being dominated. The heroine is typically a WASP English/Commonwealth girl travelling away from home. She invariably gets into some kind of trouble and is saved by the hero. While men in Mills and Boon are always sure about their love, women have to overcome obstacles to be certain of it. The Mills and Boon heroines 'often cannot remember their fathers, or they never had one'.

Of course many women read Mills and Boon as entertainment and recognise the absurdity of the stereotypes involved and the fantastic elements of exaggeration in the stories. Equally, it can be argued that the types of popular fiction and entertainment that men enjoy are just as naive and fantastic. Men escape more by fantasising about adventure, as in the war/detective stories, while women do it via romance. Cultural fantasies, however, are part of society and undoubtedly influence people's behaviour.

Escapist romanticism is mostly about love and sex. This kind of romanticism is involved in current publicity campaigns to persuade Australians that Bryan Brown and Helen Morse are 'the' couple of the eighties. Bob Ellis, one of the *enfants terrible* of the Australian intelligensia, recently tried this in an article in *Video Age*. Ellis worked himself up to a level of masturbatory fantasy trying to picture Brown/Morse as an Oz eighties version of the tragic couple of 1940s cinema like Tracy/Hepburn, Gable/Harlow, etc.

Characteristically inconsistent, Ellis knocked both stars' acting ability in the article, but concluded hysterically:

> They do their country proud. They are part of the race memory now and deservedly so... That is good to see, in these terrible earnest, defeated days we are living through. Morse and Brown are the sum of our nation's victories. (*Video Age*, November '82)

Ellis cast Morse in the role of 'the tender female aroused reluctantly', while he vicariously fantasised about Brown as 'the man who will not take no for an answer'. This is a prize example of middle-class literary ockerism.

Traditional romanticism concerns itself more with the family and conventional sex-roles. Figures like John Laws or the stylishly conventional movie presenters on Channel 0/28 convey different versions of Australian middle-class traditional romanticism. Where Macdonalds uses romantic love as a gloss to sell its products, other firms like Diamond Traders International use imagery about couples and the family as the centre-piece of their promotions.

John Laws' appeal to women is based very much on his self-presentation as a traditional romantic man. Laws has nine kids and thirteen cars. His habit of calling all women callers 'Mam', and of stressing sentimentality in his music and personal anecdotes, all endorse paternalism in conventional Australian male behaviour. The package is the same as that endorsed by Christian fundamentalism, except the wrapper is more glossy.

On the religious level traditional romanticism is supported by the Churches. Love of family is associated with love of God, and religious propaganda sheets like the American Church of God's *Plain Truth* use traditional family values as an explanatory frame of reference for world affairs. The October 1982 edition of *Plain Truth* accordingly presents political disagreements between the U.S. and Europe as a 'divorce'. It asks plaintively in another article why God lets little children die, then hammers away at international violence and terrorism versus how to have healthy babies and improve your Bible IQ. American media evangelicism of this kind has been an important influence on postwar Australia.

There is lastly the level of complex romanticism in Australian culture. Paul Wilson's book *Intimacy* is quite convincing about the fact that for many Australian men love is one of their central concerns in life. It is at this level that ideas and values about complex romanticism are important. Love is important to men because it is a way out of a life full of routine. White-collar workers are tied to bureaucracies and corporations, and blue-collar workers are tied to factory assembly lines or building sites. Given the confines of normal employment and the geographical closure of the frontier in the Western world, men can no longer go adventuring—except as tourists. The possibility of falling in love remains one of the most dramatic changes that can happen in a man's personal life.

Australian men traditionally have been heavy gamblers. Love for Australian men, on this deepest, most serious level, removed from the fantasies of admen and star-struck journalists, is such an important thing as it is one of the few times when men put their own personalities seriously at risk. The possibility of love dramatically changing a man's life is one of the few variations left on a well-programmed life.

Urban Loneliness and Media Matchmaking

The women's movement has raised issues about the suburban isolation of women as housewives, but the social isolation of significant numbers of men in Australian city life is often overlooked. It seems to be taken for granted that adult men can cope better with city life than women. Certainly they have a higher degree of physical access to city life, yet freedom and isolation go together for many city men. The Henderson Poverty Report found that elderly, single men were one of the main poverty stricken groups.

One example is the lifestyle of poorer, older men living in the inner city. Since the decline of the boarding-house as a 1950s institution, not belonging to a family has been made much harder for men. In November '82 one Sydney man staggered back to his inner-western home at a private hotel after a pub fight. Briefly noticed by one of the other residents, he went to his room where he was found dead three days later.

On a less dramatic level, routine social isolation is a problem which affects both sexes in city life. It is increasingly being commercially catered for in the growth of introduction agencies as well as media matchmaking programmes. Mike Willesee's first TV special for 1983 featured the Sydney introduction agency scene, where he went doggedly in pursuit of 'the greatest product imaginable—true love'.

The programme took a fairly light-hearted look at its subject, and set the tone by using Billie Holliday's song 'Lover Where Can You Be'. It was shown that higher-priced agencies, like Yvonne Allen and Herson and Associates, were run by women and had more women clients, where in computer dating agencies more men were involved as managers and customers. One woman interviewed referred to loneliness as 'a disease I've had all my life'. She also said she could relate to only a small percentage of average Australian men. As Willesee's only male subject on the show was English, Australian men's role in the agency world wasn't seriously considered (27 February '83).

Sydney talkback radio shows that specialise in matchmaking don't charge for their services, but they use loneliness to get an audience. Singleton includes matchmaker spots in his 2KY morning breakfast show which are typically satirical and cynical, while Brian Wiltshire's 'Midnight Matchmaker' show on 2GB is more serious.

The Midnight Matchmaker formula is for the caller to answer a list of questions put by the host about their looks, age, job, activities, and preferences for what they want in the opposite sex (there are never any gay matches made). Wiltshire does this informally with each caller.

Then at the end of the episode he recounts the caller's vital facts like an accountant adding up figures: name, age, height, and cultural serial number. Any exclusions? 'Boozers and Eyetalians', says one lady-caller who keeps greyhounds (2GB, 23 November '82).

Where 2GB's Matchmaker show is sometimes too serious, Singo's version is a flagrant send-up. Parts of his morning show are devoted to some surprisingly serious counselling sessions about unemployment and family problems, assisted by Ted Noffs and others from the Kings Cross Wayside Chapel. Most of the radio stations seems to be moving in this direction as the recession worsens. However by 11 am or so it's time to brighten things up, so Singo introduces his 'Dinner With Sally' contest, which can run for thirty minutes.

Here Sally—who is on-line somewhere else—vets a selection of potential suitors who call her live on air to persuade her to have dinner with them ... with one of them, that is. So Max from Redfern rings: '(boldly) Hello ... This is Max from Redfern ... (not-so-boldly) ... Er, could you tell me a few things about yourself Sally please?' This is after Singo has already sung Sally's praises and described her tastes in some detail. Sally (miffed): 'You've already done that John... Weren't you listening Max?'

And so on. Sally and Singo together make mincemeat out of most of the men who call in. There's a certain degree of recognition of the game-like element involved by at least some of the callers. As the number of potential suitors grows, Singo starts calling the state of play in sporting terms, illustrated with his own leaden jokes—'You a good kisser Sally?' etc. So far Sally doesn't seem to have chosen anyone. Not even Jim from Warriewood who rings every week (2KY, 25 November '82).

Single men—and also single women—in Australia traditionally have been seen as a rather suspect group. Despite the cliches about 'gay bachelors' (a pre-gay term), the Australian media and the public still tend to look askance at single adult men. 'FREE BACHELORS FIND LIFE LONELY', as one *Daily Telegraph* report put it. This item cited comments by a Melbourne woman psychologist that bachelors were lonelier than spinsters. Also that they were more likely to be lonely than married men (28 August '82).

Conducting its own instant poll, the paper asked Gordon Elliot (compere of 10's *Good Morning Australia*), Donnie Sutherland (TV rockshow host), Peter Collins (Liberal MP for Willoughby), and Russel Fairfax (League star), what they thought. Elliot and Sutherland agreed that bachelor life had its elements of loneliness and pitfalls. Collins—who was the only man identified as being separated—gave a typical politician's non-commital answer, but disagreed. Fairfax more positively suggested that single men had more friends than married men.

While the sexuality of celebrities is constantly used as a selling point by the media, the human and psychological difficulties of ordinary single men either aren't considered seriously, or are viewed negatively. Three months later Donnie Sutherland lost his licence after his third drunk-driving conviction. 'TV ROCKSTAR GUILTY OF DRINK CHARGE', said the *Telegraph* again. But this time the paper didn't mention Donnie's bachelor status at all. His manager tactfully explained that Donnie couldn't be expected to be a goody-goody. 'After all, he's a rockin' personality' (*T*, 24 November '82).

In this kind of social climate Australian men soon get the message that if they remain single they risk either being considered gay or as misfits who have missed out. 'All my friends are getting married,' sang Shirley from Skyhooks sadly in the seventies. One of the keys to full male adult status is marriage. For Australian men the taking on of full masculine identity is defined in terms of a job, a home, a mortgage, kids—i.e., a lifestyle based on material ownership and marital duty.

The effect of these family-oriented pressures on young men probably becomes most damaging to the present generation of unemployed young men. Public information about the effects of unemployment on young people is limited, but studies by the Melbourne-based Brotherhood of St Laurence shows that the unemployed young suffer from high levels of anxiety, depression, and tend to withdraw from social contact. The Australian media have contributed to the problem by periodically reinforcing the 'dole-bludger' image of young people who supposedly don't want to work.

Heterosexual Alienation

The de-personalisation of sexuality in the Australian commercial media is so widespread it's difficult to convey its scale. Depictions of violence against women continue to be central in current American films like *Blade Runner* and *The Entity*, but there is more manipulation of sexual relationships in the media than outright violence.

Australian feature films have made their own contributions to a climate of sexual alienation. Threats of violence against women were part of the two *Mad Max* films, while the *Chant of Jimmie Blacksmith* also showed women as victims of horrific violence. Less violent contemporary urban lifestyle films like *Monkey Grip*, *Caddie* and *Mouth to Mouth*, show considerable levels of unexpressed alienation between the sexes, while the more traditional bush-oriented films like *Wake in Fright*, *Sunday Too Far Away* and *Picnic at Hanging Rock* show the sexes culturally separated into two often mutually indifferent groups.

Since the seventies, advertising has been able to draw freely on a range of previously unmentionable subjects. The collected American edition of *True Confessions* summed up the decade with three stories—'My Bride is a Man' (homosexuality), 'You're Not the First Man I've Had But You're the Best' (promiscuity), and 'You'll Love Your New Daddy Kathy' (incest and child porn). Australian commercial advertisers are as astute as American and more agressive.

This kind of chauvinism comes through explicitly in some advertising in the evening press. In April '81 a *Mirror* ad for *Australian Playboy* featured Gabriella Brum, a Miss World for a day before resigning, promising full exposure. The ad went on:

> The subject is stacked with other interesting subjects too.
> —For example, there's a terrific interview with Stuart Butler, the man in Australia's nuclear hot seat.
> —You'll read how homosexuals have made Sydney the 'poof' capital of the Pacific.
> —And die laughing at an article that tells you how to survive in Afghanistan. (*M*, 2 April '81)

Anti-female, anti-gay and pro-militaristic attitudes keep recurring in Australian chauvinist advertising. On late night Sydney commercial radio, agressive chauvinism is taken for granted. Here is a piece of late night 1982 radio from 2SM (21 April '82):

Item 1 A Tia Maria commercial as a radio sketch of Murray and his girlfriend. Murray is socially inept and his girl is trying to educate him. They go to a 1950s style restaurant where some guys are wearing blue plastic pants. Murray's girl explains to him this is not unmanly, but trendy. Murray saves face by wisecracking that 'what's trendy now is old-fashioned in thirty seconds', and reaches for his Tia Maria and Coke.

Item 2 An authoritative hard-sell male voice promoting a woman's beauty product—'Babe, you just can't get enough'.

Item 3 Radio theatre used to introduce the Dial-a-Record of the week. This fantasy concerns a backyard strangler caught up in the washing line. This introduces The Stranglers new record, put to air as the DJ overdubs the intro, whispering humorously 'Strangle Your Mum'.

Commercial sound sequences like this defy objective description and carry subliminal nuances. The sequence spells out the promise (and threat) of the conventional Australian dream for teenagers—be straight, be het and romantic, get a wife and a job, live in the suburbs, go mad and kill your wife or mum. Advertisers defend such methods by claiming their fantasies are humorous and not meant to be taken seriously. However the hard sell sex/violence line is pushed by Sydney commercial music radio stations insistently at adolescents and young adults.

A greater emphasis on child porn is now also visible in Australian outdoor advertising and on TV. 'Don't Let Your Baby Grow Up to Wear Levis', warns the ad, which on TV features soft-core images of teenage whores in fantasy country and western bar scenes. As a cultural concern, it comes through in recent films about youthful innocence, like Brooke Shields in *Blue Lagoon*. When in 1981 Brooke Shields' mother was criticised by an American High Court judge for letting her daughter—then aged ten—pose in the nude, this criticism was echoed in Australian radio news comment without the media's role being considered (2UW, October '81).

The Australian commercial media's avoidance of homosexual experience—except as a joke—fosters an obsession with heterosexual romance. Unwilling to acknowledge homosexual public identity, the Australian media remain fascinated with depravity, incest and any scenario featuring sexual perversity.

The official face of the Australian media in public—at, say, the Logie Awards—is its responsible, community-service image. But its private behaviour—it's daily screen performances, that is—is more like that of a dirty old man who is foolishly preoccupied with sex. The visual media and the evening papers consistently feature sexuality (and violence) well beyond the bounds of conventional experience.

When we step back from this barrage of media misinformation about sexuality, the real elements of alienation in Australian sexual culture can be traced back to the prevalence of conventionally repressive family-based attitudes. Men's relations with Australian women concentrate first on family life and secondly on sex. There is an enormous amount of commercial media coverage of sex, but the moral framework behind much of it is one of conservative family values.

In marriage and in many courting relationships, Australian men see women as partners or possessions. Though seeing women as partners is socially acceptable in Australian culture, seeing them as possessions is much less so. Yet the first attitude is as oppressive as the second. Seeing women as partners is destructive because it identifies people primarily in materialistic terms. Since the sixties the older styles of sexual paternalism have been challenged by newer styles of indulgent autonomy and self-gratification. This is sometimes referred to as 'the new narcissism'.

However Australian materialism is not just a way of life or a simple pre-occupation with money, it is more a state of mind and feeling. Cultural attitudes of personal autonomy and openness to sex can be just as repressive as the older styles of paternalism. The calculation of personality and personal relationships in material terms reduces the value of human experience to the level of what can be counted. Relationships become what you can get out of people.

Socially, these instrumental attitudes of Australian men promote an interpersonal style of casual sexual alienation. There is a depressing taken-for-grantedness in the low levels of expectations Australian men and women hold for heterosexual intimacy. A comment by a Melbourne psychologist to the Royal Commission on Human Relationships was:

> The level of satisfaction in sexual relationships in the Australian community is extremely low. [There is] . . . a general lack of honest and meaningful sex education coupled with the problem of misleading attitudes and myths relating to sex, particularly the double standard. (HR, 3/2)

This social alienation between the sexes is the setting for the media's depersonalisation of sexuality, and the continued lack of emotional communication between Australian men and women. What is most culturally obvious is the emotional inexpressiveness of Australian men. While men publicly avoid talking about sexuality, their private behaviour to women is often likely to be ignorant, romantic, and tough.

Apathy is one of the worst problems in Australian heterosexual culture. This is the particular form of violence which has permeated Australian interpersonal relations between the sexes—a sense of resentment and negative aggression, where emotional passivity is the norm for men and aggression is the release. Rape and domestic violence are serious Australian social problems, but the more deep-seated social malaise they grow out of is the sense of estrangement and withdrawal between Australian men and women which is largely taken for granted. The media, in turn, worsen this insecurity by using fears about sexual and social identity to sell products and win ratings.

7 Anti-Social Sex and the Media

Prostitution, porn and rape are anti-social sexual activities which indicate an increasing degree of alienation between the sexes. For men, each is a step further away from the achievement of mutual intimacy with a woman. Men who pay for sex at least are still choosing to be with women, whereas men who rape are suffering from complete sexual alienation. Yet although Australians view these anti-social forms of sex with official disfavour, it also extends degrees of toleration to them. Prostitution is becoming decriminalised and porn is more tolerated. There is no official toleration of rape, yet public attitudes still often blame the victim.

The media's treatment of anti-social sex is part of this wider social problem. It periodically pays attention to prostitution, and—to a lesser extent—rape, but the commercial display of sexuality is an important part of the visual media. TV advertising, especially, sexually objectifies women, endorses traditional sex-role separation, and male sexual aggressiveness. At the same time, some media programs about sex attempt to educate the public about changing moral standards.

Prostitution: 'What's A Nice Girl Like You...

The degree of disapproval Australians are likely to express of prostitution depends on where it takes place. Prostitution in Sydney now is upfront and out on the streets, where in Melbourne it centres around massage parlours. Sydney's street-walkers, however, are still being subjected to strong protests by Darlinghurst residents who are concerned about ethics and real estate prices.

The media foreground the criminal, legal, and moral sides of prostitution. The quality Sydney press, for instance, tends to foreground criminal and legal arguments, while the evening papers and the broadcast media emphasise its shock/amusement value. Sensationalist media treatment of prostitution projects either or both a sense of moral outrage and salacious enjoyment of the issue. To consider the broadcast media's attitudes I want to discuss ABC TV and radio treatment of the subject. Here the ABC tends to reflect commercial media attitudes in a slightly lower key.

In November 1982 ABC TV ran a special called 'What's A Nice Girl Like You?' on *Four Corners* (21 November '82). Prior to this, the programme was previewed on 2BL's *City Extra* on the preceding Monday. There Margaret Throsby talked with Peter Ross, the main reporter on the TV special, and with 'Robin', one of the girls in the show. Essentially, Throsby conducted a sympathetic and critical discussion of the issue, whereas Peter Ross—a middle-aged, conservatively dressed and spoken man in the ABC's Melbourne style—took a conventional line.

Throsby used the issue to inform her radio listeners about the whys and hows of prostitution, without the heavy-handed moral judgements made in the TV show. She drew Robin out to make useful comments, such as those about Australian men who went to prostitutes. Robin estimated that one-quarter of her customers were respectable young men in their mid-twenties. She claimed that she had a de facto counselling relationship with some customers, and that prostitution was a safety valve for many men in unsatisfying marriages.

On the other hand, liberal statements in an overall conservative media context like the ABC are invariably co-opted or undermined by other programming or presentational techniques. Throsby let Ross restate allegations made by an unidentified policeman about how 98 per cent of girls on Melbourne's St Kilda Road beat were on hard drugs, and that some had a $2500-a-day habit.

Throsby also referred conventionally to the 'unsavoury world of hookers and drugs at the Cross', and took no phone calls on the subject at the end of the discussion. Her treatment of the subject had been preceded by the 9 am news, which had carried a report from Bernard Mays in New York about the supposed 'epidemic' of sexually transmitted disease claimed to be afflicting American gays. The lesson, concluded Mays, was 'cool off and stay at home'.

On the *Four Corners*' version only male reporters were used. Ross' traditional, authoritative statements were supplemented and made less boring by the comments of a younger and ostentatiously street-wise journalist. 'Street girls do it as they've always done it,' he said knowingly at the start of the show, 'the reasons haven't changed.' The show concluded with Ross patronisingly asking one woman 'How can you make prostitution respectable?'

The programme showed only one male customer on screen, identified another verbally as 'a Greek businessman from Wollongong', and showed just one protector. These men were presented as misguided or crooked. The customer shown was a young, respectably-dressed well-spoken man, who was treated with puzzled curiosity by Ross. Answering the question about why he paid for sex, he stated that he wanted good looks, intelligence and charm, and a good bed partner as well. It was simpler to pay for this instead of wasting time searching. This response is a good example of Australian men's confusion of directness and innocence in dealing with women.

The one protector shown was framed as a dodgy character. He was shot with his back to the camera, awkwardly evading questions about the nature of his 'gentlemen's club' in Melbourne. In contrast, the reporters themselves and policemen were shown as the heroes. Policemen were treated with respect as considerate men doing an unpleasant job. While Ross made no comment on one constable's claim that some St Kilda girls were spending thousands of dollars a day on drugs, the one item on the show where a girl complained of police brutality and rape was de-emphasised by an off-camera reporter's comment about 'serious unsubstantiated allegations'.

Most TV shows about social issues carry dominant and secondary meanings. ABC TV's dominant approach to controversial issues is to reproduce conventional morality, but also to place a secondary emphasis on the presentation of slightly subversive material. This is done for several reasons. One is to keep the show reasonably interesting and to say something to viewers who aren't conventionally conservative; another is to approximate to the traditional, vague, liberal ideal of ABC 'balanced treatment'; a third is a conscious strategy on the part of a small minority of the ABC's staff who support social reform.

The dominant meaning of 'What's a Nice Girl Like You?' was to ask conventional moral questions about prostitution—why and how do people do it? And, implicitly, should and how can we stop it? The secondary meaning of both the TV and radio versions was different— how do we make prostitution respectable? The TV version raised the second question by stressing the family side of prostitution. The show began with a reference to what their mothers would think of these girls, and later included footage of an Adelaide 'madam' and her daughter who'd also been 'on the game'. Conventional morality of course has associated prostitution with drugs, crime and depravity for years. What was more notable about this cycle of ABC attention to the subject, however, was the extent to which it suggested prostitution was a form of Australian family life gone wrong.

Porn: TV Advertising as Soft-Core Porn

Fantasy is one of the central experiences for modern city people. In an urbanised, car-dominated, and physically confined environment, shared fantasy about the subject matter of films, TV, radio and print media is a crucial part of city people's cultural experience. Porn is dangerous in this image-rich environment because it reduces fantasy to obsession, just as advertising reduces TV to a commercial propaganda machine. Porn impoverishes men's imaginations, just as a repressive boarding school upbringing constricts children's emotions.

Porn seems to be for some men what romance is for women—a means of escapism and entertainment on a superficial level, but with the potential for a more serious use of fantasy to act as a means of psychological self-definition. Where traditionally women have used men to define their social identity by forming dependent–submissive relationships, men have used sex more as a means of self-discovery.

Contemporary arguments in Sydney about porn often revolve around film censorship. In the 1982 film festival an unsuccessful—and unwarranted—censorship attempt was made on *Pixote*, a Brazilian film. As part of its wider theme about the exploitation of the urban poor, the film had shown a sex scene involving children. Some argument also took place around the Opera House screening of *Not a Love Story*, a Canadian women's anti-porn film about the porn trade. Another 1982 controversy was over the removal of Juan Davila's paintings from an art gallery during the Bienniale of Sydney. The paintings had shown graphic images of gay sex.

The problem in debating porn is that hard-line feminists and conservative religious groups both oppose porn, if for different reasons. The dilemma is to be critical of porn without supporting puritanism or censorship. As English feminist Angela Carter has suggested, there may well be a case to be made for a moral or pro-social pornography. Art has always used sex—and anything else it can—to shock people into awareness of wider levels of experience, and it should continue to do so.

But this is probably too sophisticated a way of talking about porn for most Australians. Where prostitution reduces intimacy to depersonalised sexual encounters, conventional porn reduces intimacy to the level of privatised fantasy. In both cases there is a narrowing of social experience, which leads to greater levels of personal alienation.

Another difficulty in talking about porn is that apart from the ambiguous distinction between hard and soft-core porn, many critics haven't looked at porn seriously enough to make sense of it. One piece of Sydney graffiti says that eroticism is the pornography of the rich, but it makes as much sense to say that porn is the eroticism of the poor. More seriously, porn can be classified in the same way as romanticism—there's vulgar, naive, escapist and traditional porn. Vulgar porn is soft-core and based more on male narcissistic fantasies, while traditional porn is hard-core and comes from male fantasies about sado-masochism.

Vulgar porn uses images of instant sex. As vulgar romanticism relies on artificial love, vulgar porn relies on artificial, trivial sex. It is most often seen in soft-core Australian TV advertising. Sex is often so irrelevant to many of the products it's meant to sell it's ridiculous. The Moove flavoured milk and Flake chocolate bar ads are exemplars.

The Moove ad (Big M in Victoria) uses a series of stunning special-effects and a pop sound track to visually consume a pretty girl stranded on an Eden-like beach. The camera takes voyeuristic pleasure in close-ups of her body, and the loose association of health and sexiness is made with flavoured milk. The Flake ad is more sexually explicit. It focuses on a young couple doing teasingly exciting things with a chocolate bar on an island paradise location. Both ads hint at a lost Eden-like existence, touching on old Christian archetypes. Young kids don't consciously know that the chocolate bar in the Flake ads is being presented subliminally as a phallus, but advertisers do.

When reform groups try to pressure advertisers about these types of ads, the agencies respond that such criticisms are based on 'subjective judgements of taste and decency'. The Australian Consumer's Association (ACA)—publishers of *Choice* magazine—surveyed Sydney TV advertising in October 1981, looking especially at the promotion of junk foods, alcohol advertising, and the stereotyping of women and minority groups.

They found a saturation of children's viewing time with ads for nutritionally dubious products, as well as heavy alcohol advertising in the 7.30 to 8.30 time-slot. Ads for junk foods pressure kids into the 'eat fast—eat sweet' syndrome, while the placement of alcohol ads after 7.30 still reaches many children under 13, as adult-only programmes cannot be shown before 8.30. This goes against the recommendations of a Senate Standing Committee in 1981 on TV and Children's Behaviour that was adamant that alcohol advertising should not be shown before 9 pm (ACA, 1982).

Predictably, the ACA study also showed consistent stereotyping of women in a sexist manner. Their description of a B&D roll-a-door ad: 'Boy lewdly staring at a girl while a man describes the B&D roll-a-door as "slim styling in centre left lock ... so good it won the Australian Design Award," is not in good taste'. The Federation of Australian Commercial Television's (FACTS) response here was the 'subjective judgement of taste and decency' reply. FACTS referred to the view of Sir Richard Kirby (Chairman of the Advertising Standards Council) who had claimed that it would be difficult, if not impossible, to define suitable codes to embrace such a complex area as taste and decency.

A second type of soft-core porn is naive porn. Where vulgar porn is about ersatz sex, naive porn is about plain, straight sex. Where vulgar porn is ridiculous, naive porn—as in *Playboy*—is often silly and juvenile. *Australian Playboy* uses the same ingredients as the Hefner original—a featured interview with a distinguished man (Graham Greene), a current affairs article on Oz politics (Craig McGregor), a feature article on sports ('Why the Stars of World Tennis Hate Each Others Guts'), as well as the usual banal and innocent array of pin-up girls and Miss Centrefold. *Playboy*, compared to *Australian Penthouse*, is mild stuff. Its particular brand of naive porn is aimed at young, sexually inexperienced men, or those little-boys-who-never-grow-up type of middle-aged men.

Escapist porn moves away from soft towards hard-core porn. It is more sophisticated and is concerned to express eroticism rather than just sex. Where escapist romanticism revolved around love and sex fantasies grounded in narcissism, the images of escapist porn are tied more to auto-eroticism. Australian current affairs magazine *The Bulletin* uses escapist porn peripherally in its advertising. *The Bulletin* is very much a 'thinking man's' magazine aimed at an older and more educated market than *Playboy* or *Penthouse*. When sexuality is used in the magazine's ads it's something of an afterthought. Women are presented here just as a temporary escape: one ad promotes a calendar book by Patrick Lichfield, featuring the rear view of a pretty hitch-hiker with her bum exposed as well as her legs. Another ad for Barlow sailboards shows a topless girl with a mask-like face gazing sightlessly at the sailboards.

But escapist porn is peripheral to *The Bulletin*. It's more central in another, newer Sydney magazine, *Billy Blue*. This is a North Sydney based, trendy mag for young adults, especially in the business, marketing and advertising trades. It has excellent production values, a stylish layout, and is sexually explicit in its use of escapist porn. One March 1981 copy was labelled 'a special salacious issue', where its lead fiction story was a sexual fantasy called 'The Kid'.

This was a story about a young woman working in a 'boring petty little job' who lives out her fantasies by seducing a schoolboy. The story is written by a woman, and well written. The heroine rather comically seduces the boy by first offering him lollies, then—1980s style—hash. The story is told as a power struggle between her and the boy, who finally gives her VD. Though the story verges on being genuine social comment, it cashes in on the current wave of prurient interest in children's sexuality (*Blue Lagoon*), and ultimately depersonalises both characters.

Rape As Forcible Seduction

Some feminists, such as Germaine Greer and Ann Summers, have taken a very hard line against men's responsibility for rape. They argue it is a political act which men use to consolidate their traditional domination over women. My response to this is that rape is not just an anti-female act, but an anti-human one. Men have raped other men in Australian prisons. There are also recorded Australian cases of women arranging revenge rapes, or physically assisting in the rape of other women. Child sexual abuse is also a threat to young boys as well as girls.

Rape may arise as much from men's estrangement from other men, as from a need to express their solidarity with each other. Men commit rape not so much out of a conscious intention to re-assert patriarchal authority, as from confusion and misery arising out of a lack of involvement in supportive social networks in the first place. Men who rape, like men who beat their wives and children, probably do so from an overwhelming sense of frustration and anger at not being able to cope with the conventional norms of Australian heterosexual culture.

Australian and overseas figures suggest that rape offenders are most likely to be young, working-class men. But the significance of this finding is equivocal. The mechanics of the Australian criminal justice system are class-biased in the first place. Paul Wilson, in his 1979 pro-feminist book *The Other Side of Rape*, has suggested that middle-class men commit rape as often. But they are less likely to have had their crimes reported or detected in the first place, and more likely to have greater resources to evade or fight prosecution.

The more traditional view about men who rape still seems justified—with one major qualification. Working-class men are more likely to be alienated from the cultural mainstream than middle-class men. They are therefore more prone to committing anti-social crimes such as rape, assault and armed robbery. Young men who grow up in culturally-deprived working class suburbs are likely to have less tolerant and more aggressive attitudes to personal interaction. Men brought up in more affluent areas like Sydney's North Shore are less likely to see the city as a jungle. Phillips' 1979 study of the attitudes of Sydney school-kids provides evidence of this.

Mainstream Australian commercial culture, however, is run by middle-class men. The men in senior and line positions in advertising and the media come from higher class backgrounds, or have acquired that status and set of attitudes in the course of their careers. The aggressive sexist culture pushed by the Australian media creates a middle-class, white, male fantasy world about personal relationships which sees personal manipulation as part of everyday behaviour. When *Australian Playboy* carries a cartoon showing a presumably adulterous wife, dressed in sexy black bra and stockings, crying out 'Rape! Rape!' as her husband comes home unexpectedly, it is playing on Australian men's cynicism about women and contributing to a climate of sexual distrust and hostility (December '82).

Wilson, Summers and other writers have attempted to classify different types of rape according to different circumstances. Most of these redefinitions, however, have looked at rape solely from a woman's viewpoint. If instead rape is seen as a form of anti-social sexuality, then it must be considered along with other negative forms of sexual interaction, such as sexual manipulation, sexual harassment, sexual molestation, as well as legally-defined rape.

Sue Rhodes' 1967 book *Now You'll Think I'm Awful* talked about the high levels of manipulation prevalent in ordinary Australian heterosexual contact. Attitudes have improved since then, but Australian men and women still can be ruthless in the way they use sex and power as bargaining mechanisms in their intimate relationships. Some of these kinds of sexual manipulation were re-labelled by Greer and Summers as rape by fraud and petty rape. Their point was that Australian men both trick and trap women for sexual purposes.

Cases of this kind usually only become public when one of the offended parties seeks legal redress. One 1981 example concerned a young, attractive, counter-cultural man who'd become one of Sydney's lower-North-Shore Don Juans. In return for sexual and material favours he'd become engaged to some seventeen women, until finally one had taken legal action to recover her property. Another example was of a middle-aged Eastern Suburbs socialite who'd seduced a woman by promising her that several Hollywood stars would be at the wedding, which hadn't taken place.

This kind of sexual deceit and manipulation is not just practiced by Australian men. It's more a negative feature of Australian sexual culture generally, at which women are just as bad and good as men. Australian women cope with men's sexism and aggression by employing negative forms of aggression of their own. Women get used to saying 'no' sexually in Australia, and they use passivity, snobbery, humiliation, scorn, and other indirect means of emotional control to make men believe it. Women are forced into doing this because they are mostly in weaker material positions than men, and consequently more open to exploitation.

At points the media system overlaps sufficiently with private life for these values to be visible. Father Jim McLaren's Sunday night counselling talkback session on radio 2UE is one example. Here personal manipulation is encouraged in terms of Christian morality. Most of 'Father Jim's' callers tend to be young women or adolescents who are feeling unhappy, guilty or isolated in dealing with a personal problem. Many, by their speech patterns, are working- or lower-middle-class people.

Father Jim takes it for granted that every normal person wants love, romance, and a family as a matter of course. He rarely advises people to be independent and different rather than dependent and conformist. One worried sixteen-year-old girl called him, for example, to explain that now her boyfriend was eighteen he could go to pubs and discos where she couldn't. She was afraid that her boyfriend would now find another girl to replace her.

Father Jim's response was that (a) she shouldn't be worried if he really loved her, and (b) she shouldn't confront her boyfriend directly about this, but tell him instead that she trusted him! In other words, be manipulative instead of open (12 December '82). This is an objectively trivial example, but it illustrates perfectly the negative sense of heterosexual relationships as a competition which many Australians seem to accept as normal.

Sexual harassment is the next step up the ladder leading towards rape. Though sexual harassment is now being defined more in terms of sexual manipulation and discrimination on the job, this form of negative personal interaction also extends to behaviour on the streets and any public place. Sexual harassment in this broader sense happens to women at a range of different occasions—at rock concerts and festivals, at nude and ordinary beaches, and for pretty girls walking along city streets. In October '82 the national pop music magazine *Ram* carried a feature specifically warning girls about the risks of rape at pop concerts.

Direct sexual molestation short of rape is the next stage. This can be passive, as with peeping toms and male flashers or masturbators on public transport, or active in terms of the different forms of sexual assault short of rape. One study of Victorian sex offenders in 1975 showed that more men were in prison for these offenses than for rape—carnal knowledge, indecent assault, incest, gross indecency, and buggery and bestiality (Bush, 1977).

With legally defined rape three versions are most common—gang rape, rape by lone strangers, and child abuse. Men who become involved in gang rapes often belong to sub-cultural groups which have aggressive codes of masculinity, such as group sex ceremonies. Cases such as the notorious gang rapes which occurred at Ingham, North Queensland, in 1977 were based on this kind of male bonding. Gang rape there was referred to as 'training' the local girls. Media treatment of the Ingham cases, however, tended to write them off as just another Queensland aberration (*NT*, 16 April '81).

The Murdoch evening press, however, continues to use news about anti-social sex, especially rape, as a sales device. A regular ingredient of sensationalist sex crime coverage is the association of one item with other 'news' about sex in the paper's general layout. In one issue of the *Mirror* which headlined 'TERROR ATTACKS ON FOUR YOUNG GIRLS', around a series of sexual assaults in Sydney's southern suburbs, another item was carried about the expulsion of two women students from the Australian Union of Students reportedly because they didn't 'go along with the theory that all men are rapists'. Between these items on pages 3 and 11 respectively, on page 7 the *Mirror* headlined the 'PICK OF THE PETS', about the 1983 *Penthouse* Pet of the Year contest (3 February '83). The cultural association between seduction and rape in the popular press, that is, produces sensationally distorted news coverage about rape. Rape is seen as little more than forcible seduction.

8 Family Men—Men and Family Life

More Australians are marrying now than ever before. The 1977 Royal Commission on Human Relationships described the postwar marriage trend as one of 'almost universal marriage'. Marriage is seen by many as a social inevitability. Since 1967, however, the extension of birth control and the rise in numbers of women working have reduced the national birth rate. Families are smaller. Before 1914 average family size was about twice what it has become after 1945. The probability of divorce also has risen dramatically—by 200 per cent between 1900 and 1967 (HR, 4/8). This paradox of increased rates of marriage as well as of divorce in Australia has led to wide debate about the family's future.

There has since been greater recognition of the prevalence of domestic violence in Australian families regardless of their class, and some acknowledgement that the emotional needs of men in family conflicts are largely unknown. What I want to argue is that routine male socialisation in Australian families produces men who are tough, competitive, aggressive and prone to initiating violence, but that this affects working-class families most.

Men and Families

In 1979, speaking at a South Australian conference on family conflict, sociologist Anna Yeatman raised the question why interpersonal conflict in Australian families was usually so destructive. If conflict in the family took place between equals, Yeatman suggested, it need not necessarily always lead to trouble, but 'commonsense and professional experience' testified to the usually destructive nature of such conflict—that amicable divorce was a rarity.

Her main conclusion was that conflict between men and women in

Australian families was socially patterned:

> It seems to me that there is only one fact which can account for this socially-patterned, destructive aspect of conflict between men and women. This factor is, simply, the persistence of inequality in the status and power of women relative to those of men in the family, when, at the same time, women have been led to expect they have a legitimate claim to the same rights as men. (Yeatman, 85)

The basic cultural contradiction for women in modern families, then, is that though the sexual division of labour in the public domain—especially the work-place—is breaking down, it still persists within marriage. Housework and child-raising are still seen as women's jobs, not men's. Further, jobs in the public domain which appear related to domestic work—primary and pre-school teaching, social work, and nursing—are seen as still belonging to women. This contradiction produces personal and social problems. Personally, it creates value conflicts, role confusion and ambivalence; socially, it leads to resource problems about the lack of adequate child-care facilities.

Yeatman's analysis is important as it addresses the issue of family class differences in experiencing conflict. Working-class men, she argues, appear to accept and expect patriarchal rights and powers more unquestioningly; but middle-class, especially professional men, tend to dispute the legitimacy of male dominance in general, yet rationalise their assertion of it in their own marriages.

Here she cites American research about the way middle-class men uphold the double standard in marriage. They no longer advocate male domination in principle—as working-class men are traditional and naive enough to do—but they still practice it. Professional men instead insist that their families should not interfere with their work. The professional husband claims preferential treatment not because he is head of the family, or male, but because he is a professional. 'By contrast, lower-class men demand deference as men, as heads of families.' (Yeatman, 87)

Most of the recent writing on Australian families, however, has been produced by women. It's important to also consider men's arguments about the subject. To do this, I want to mention Ronald Conway's theories about the absence of positive fathering roles in Australian families, then relate this back to Yeatman's argument about the class dimensions of sexual role conflict within family life.

In his first book in 1970 Conway cited findings that Australian women held most of the decision-making power within the home. The American researcher who'd originally made this finding was so impressed with Australian women's dominance in the home—not in public—he coined the term 'matriduxy' to describe it. Recent research findings about parental roles in decision making, however, are not as clear about this.

In his most recent book Conway makes more qualifications about the issue, yet still re-states the view that Australian families typically suffer from parental deprivation. He discusses different types of modern Australian marriage—marriages of convenience, of romantic intimacy, of friendship, and narcissistic and sadistic marriages—but concludes by repeating his thesis about the importance of the absent father. 'The impression in both Australia and the U.S. is that the fathers tend to be passive and less influential at the upper end of the social spectrum and most punitive or neglectful at the lower end' (Conway, 56).

Where Yeatman is stressing the negative effect of power inequalities between husband and wife, Conway is concentrating on the effects of the father's absence on children. They agree in identifying significant class differences in Australian family experiences. I now want to take up the issue of male socialisation in families, and incorporate both Yeatman's emphasis on family role conflicts and Conway's stress on absent fathers within a class and cultural context.

Boys learn to be men in a variety of increasingly complex social environments—through the family, the peer group, through schools, the media, and the organisations they eventually work in. Though studies of socialisation in tribal societies suggests there is nothing inherently biological in the family sex roles children learn, studies of industrial societies show that the absence of the father and the greater stringency of sex-role demands made on boys are crucial parts of male child raising.

Commands to boys to act like boys are levied at an earlier age than equivalent demands on girls, but usually are made in generalised, non-specific terms. Meanwhile the cultural demands of industrialism push the father out of the home and pull the mother and children back into it. Boys are expected to pattern themselves on correct styles of masculine behaviour earlier than girls, while at the same time they are denied clear models of masculinity because of the father's absence. In this way, male socialisation in industrial cultures creates an initial double-bind about identity causing tension and anxiety among boys.

The father's absence from the home during infancy and early childhood is one of the first and perhaps the most decisive event in gender formation. The father as a role model is an outline lacking most details for his sons, where the mother is more of a detailed map for her daughters. A boy's subsequent identification with his masculine role tends to be more diffuse; masculinity is first defined as that which is not feminine, and secondly as that which is not homosexual.

Because of the traditional sex role divisions dominant in child-raising in industrial societies—until at least the 1950s—the formation of the male child's sexual identity is more difficult, ambiguous and takes longer to achieve. Masculine identity also remains more tenuous throughout the male life-cycle. There is now a growing realisation of the crisis points which men experience as adolescents, in mid-life, and in their own lead-up to senescence, which is described as the male menopause. In recognition of this greater insecurity of male identity, Margaret Mead once observed that the recurrent problem of civilisation was to define the male role satisfactorily enough.

Boys are traditionally placed under more pressure in families than girls. Certain elements of tension and conflict are crucial in personality formation for both sexes, but a male specialisation in violence is encouraged through cultural conditioning. This is done by both physical punishment and psychological pressures. Psychologically, children are placed in double-bind situations by their parents to control their behaviour. In routine child-raising children are told not do something, and at the same time not talk about it.

Because of the circumstances of child-raising in traditional industrial societies, which is mostly left to women, these paradoxical commands are levelled more often and more frequently at boys than at girls. There is nothing biological in this—it is due to traditional cultural expectations. These parental commands create internal conflict—which is expressed in feelings of guilt and being blocked—and make boys more committed to competition and conflict as a means of solving problems. The individual result for sensitive boys is personality disorder, but the objective social outcome is the inculcation of culturally 'normal' competitive and aggressive attitudes as central parts of masculine identity.

Masculine aggression and competitiveness, that is, originate in routine socialisation practices. And although the establishment of gender identity precedes class identity for both boys and girls, the imprinting of class identity then reinforces the particular construction of sexuality according to existing cultural standards.

It is harder, individually, for a boy to be socialised into a masculine identity. Girls, on the other hand, are more easily socialised into feminine identity. This is so only because existing cultural values set expectations lower for girls than for boys. It may be individually harder to be a man in an existential sense, but collectively it is more difficult to be a woman, as women are a socially subordinate group.

There is a greater amount of distance—emotionally, cognitively, and socially—between personality and identity for men, and less for women. Men are taught, actively, to look outside themselves in dealing with the world, where women are encouraged to be more passive and inward. Men's violence is then projected externally, as in higher male rates of violent crime and murder; in contrast, women's violence is turned back on themselves, as in higher female rates for suicide attempts and chronic depression.

The use of language to control behaviour in family socialisation is crucially important. English socio-linguist Bernstein suggests that middle-class families are likely to be both person-centred and to develop more competent, context-free language skills among their children—that they will use an elaborated language code. By contrast, working-class families are more likely to be position-centred (Father is treated as Father, more than as a person), and to develop context-tied restricted language codes which are of more limited social prestige and utility.

Where working-class families traditionally use physical force to discipline their children, middle-class families rely more heavily on verbal argument and reasoning. This gives the middle-class child a wider communicative repertoire which improves his chances of success in the educational contests to come. It also acts as a form of long-run insurance against the manipulative language which is so widely used in a business-dominated, consumer-oriented society, especially in the media.

Some of the ways in which Australian family conflict has been class-patterned have been explored in Claire Williams' study of working-class family life in Queensland mining towns. She argues that working-class families are more vulnerable to interpersonal conflict, and to the prevalence of traditional patterns of male dominance in family life.

Williams found that working-class husbands revealed less of themselves emotionally to their wives and reacted to marriage conflict by withdrawal. Working-class men typically turned to other men for personal interests, and looked to women for comfort and understanding. Working-class men, she argues, suffered from a trained incapacity to disclose their feelings. Typically, when family disputes occurred, wives would turn to their husbands, friends, or go shopping. Husbands took refuge in other activities, drinking, or in trips away.

Williams argues that what she calls 'proletarian anti-feminism', or male working-class chauvinism, is a vital cultural defence for men against exploitation in their work environment, which is then carried back to the home. The happiest working-class marriages were those where wives had traditionally subservient relations to their husbands in family decision making. Endorsing American research on working-class families, she concluded that the ideal of masculinity inhibits expressiveness, both directly in its emphasis on personal reserve, and indirectly by identifying personal communication with the feminine role (Williams, 132).

This routinisation of aggression in ordinary child socialisation affects both working- and middle-class boys, but middle-class families have more emotional and social resources to cope with external pressures and internal conflicts. Because of their culturally dominant class position, middle-class boys find it easier to take on work roles where their aggression is positively re-defined as initiative and enterprise.

Working-class men don't have the same options to express their aggression constructively. There is instead a stress in working-class culture on associating manliness with physical strength, sport, and anti-intellectual and anti-expressive attitudes. Male working-class aggression is not culturally accepted as legitimate in the public domain, except in sports, and paternalistic male behaviour remains stronger in traditional working-class families.

The more immediate postwar cultural changes in the relations between the sexes also have affected men differently according to their class position. Before the 1960s men were expected to be tough at work, but caring husbands and fathers at home. With the effects of the women's movement, and with the greater experience of women in the work force, Australian women generally now have begun to incorporate the tougher attitudes of the public domain.

For working-class men there is less psychological distance between their traditional work and home roles. They are expected to be tough at work and strong paternal figures at home. However economic pressures now have pushed working-class women out to work. This has challenged the working-class man's traditional identity as sole breadwinner and head of the family.

More of a distinction exists between middle-class men's home and work roles. Their competitiveness at work is expected to alternate with a lower-profile, more partnership-oriented attitude at home. Middle-class men are therefore less immediately threatened by the current renegotiation of male identity at the level of family power relations between the sexes, because of the likelihood that middle-class women will have chosen to go to work instead of having been forced to. At yet another level, through their greater exposure to current cultural arguments, middle-class men are perhaps more pressured.

That generally the pressures on working-class men are greater, however, is suggested by a range of social indicators such as higher working-class crime rate, and the higher occurrence of domestic violence in working-class families on a systematic basis. Divorce is more likely to affect middle-class families, but systematic physical abuse of women is more likely to happen in working-class domestic life.

Men and Family Conflict

The less pleasant side of the conventional 'happy families' image of Australian marriage is the experience of divorce and domestic violence. These unromantic sides of family life are often treated as separate social problems as if they were not typical of 'normal' marriages. Considering the rigid sexual division of labour in conventional marriages, however, and the routinisation of aggression in male child raising, it is more realistic to see divorce and domestic violence as integral parts of the marriage experience. Family conflict is a routine part of marriage, just as industrial conflict is in work.

The increasing rate of divorce in postwar Australia does not necessarily indicate any increase in real marital breakdown. As the divorce rate has risen the separation rate has declined. More marriages that have broken up are now ending in divorce than separation. Further, about 75 per cent of divorcees re-marry.

Divorce was unusual in Australia until World War II, as in Britain. The traditional legal processes of divorce were expensive, slow and punitive. Postwar attitude changes to divorce, however, culminated in the passage of a no-fault divorce law by the Whitlam Government in 1975. Australian divorce rates today are significantly lower than American but are increasing. Marriage is certainly no longer seen as necessarily a lifetime affair, and a significant minority of people are choosing not to marry at all.

Ailsa Burns' book *Breaking Up* sheds some light on what happens to men in divorce. Single fathers made up 11 per cent of lone parents in Australia in 1975, or one in every hundred families. These fathers were relatively well-off financially compared with single mothers, and seemed to have other advantages. Some single fathers considered themselves more sensitive to others because of their experience, placed less priority on their jobs, and were more understanding of women. On the other hand, fathers who divorced without keeping some custodial links with their children were more likely to be depressed and bitter about the past (Burns, 144).

Burns also found significant class differences in the experience of divorce for men. Middle-class men were more likely to continue to take an active interest in parenting, while working-class men weren't. Men with lower levels of income and education, as Burns describes them, were more inclined to make a complete break with their family. They also were more likely to feel that their wives had turned their children against them, and to be angry about being pursued for maintenance.

This doesn't mean that divorced men generally coped better than women—father-parented families still are relatively unusual. Burns concluded that men seem to suffer most:

> For both men and women, unsuccessful marriage, separation, and divorce are painful and stressful experiences. However it is the men in this group who present the consistently more negative picture. They were more likely to feel that their standard of living had fallen since separation; to be lonely; to have found the adjustment to separation difficult; to regret the separation, and to have wanted a reconciliation, and to be interested in re-marriage. (Burns, 179)

But if Australian men suffer more from divorce than women, their roles in domestic violence are reversed. This is true at least in physical terms—what the psychological effects of domestic violence are on men as aggressors have not been investigated in Australia.

Since the mid-seventies increasing public concern has developed about domestic violence. 'Family violence is common in Australian society,' said the Royal Commission on Human Relationships, 'it cuts across lines of class, race, and sex.' Community attitudes to family violence, however, are like those towards rape—both are seen as age-old problems and each has a tacit degree of public acceptance.

The Commission was concerned to deny that domestic violence was purely a working-class problem, as has been traditionally believed. More recent studies also have reiterated that domestic violence is not exclusively a working-class family problem, but does occur in middle-class families. There is still evidence, however, that working-class wives are more liable to stay in situations where they have been regularly abused. Burns' survey reported higher attributions of cruelty (milder behaviour than assault, including mental cruelty) in the families of semi-skilled and unskilled workers.

The Commission also clearly identified alcohol and unemployment as regularly being linked with family violence, and included poverty and inadequate housing as contributing factors. It said that working class families were more vulnerable to family violence (HR, 4/139). Last, Allan's study of family violence in N.S.W. between 1880 and 1930 concluded that economically dependent wives of all classes were vulnerable to violence. Middle-class family violence, however, was more likely to arise over particular issues, rather than being a long-term feature of the relationship as it often was in working class families (O'Donnell, 19). In short, there are important qualitative differences in Australian class patterns of domestic violence, with working-class families getting the worst of it.

I have concentrated on two dimensions of men's place in contemporary Australian families—the reproduction of aggressive male identities through routine methods of child raising, and the fundamental class differences in Australian family life. Women play a central role in each of these, as dependent mothers and battered wives, yet middle- and working-class women are in very different power situations.

The most important issue is the conditions of male child raising. As already argued, in industrial societies the sexual division of labour leaves the parenting of young children to women. This is the essential precondition of the imprinting of aggression in boys. Interestingly, father absence is also considered to be one of the causes—I emphasise 'one'—of homosexuality in men. In this sense, the aggression that chauvinist men sometimes direct at homosexuals can be taken as an expression of their repressed anger at their own fathers' failure to play a larger part in their lives.

American poet Dorothy Dinnerstein has maintained that women and men ultimately come to accept the authority of patriarchal society as preferable to feminine authority. Because women are left exclusively in charge of infants and young children, both boys and girls are initially dominated by women.

In reaction to this, because of the general cultural downgrading of the importance of child-raising (e.g. the denial of women's housework as being of economic value) both sexes come to prefer the dominance of male culture as a means of ordering the world. It is seen as a lesser evil than that of their original maternal dependence. Her solution for male violence—and women's repression—is to change the conditions of child care so that men will be equally involved in active parenting roles for young children.

The immediate prospects for this kind of change in present day Australia aren't bright. Despite some moves towards role-reversal and house-husband parenting in mainly middle-class marriages, many Australian men are still distanced from their children. Demands on men about jobs and career survival are also increasing with the recession. Yet the attitude that men should be involved in active parenting is now much more widely accepted. Dinnerstein's proposal is so far the most constructive option that a radical feminist writer has put forward for men.

A second issue is the unequal distribution of social pressure on working-class families, which range from unemployment to the cultural levels of family de-personalisation touched on previously. There are in reality sharp class differences in Australian family experiences, both in conveying family authority and in coping with conflict. However the public representation of the Australian family in the media, as will be shown in the next chapter, glosses over serious differences in family resources in coping with problems, while projecting idealised pro-elite images of happy family figures.

9 Australian Families and the Media

The family is a constant source of reference for the metropolitan evening press, women's magazines and television. It is less central, but still present, in the framing styles of radio and the quality press. Mostly, family life is presented as an axiomatic good, while real or fantasy threats to the family are the recurrent source of much media sensationalism. In contrast to the complexity of the nature of real family problems, the media's treatment of the family is romantically simplistic.

The Promise of Family Life

The commercial media's representation of the family creates a symbolic picture of a world full of elite happy families, including the Royals, the wealthy and powerful, and top entertainers. This elite is overseas and domestic—links between the two are important as a means of identifying Australia's legitimate place in the world. One of the oldest English card games was 'Happy Families', where Mr Bone was the Butcher, along with Mrs Bone, Master Bone and Mistress Bone. The typologies of social relationships in that card game recur in the media's representation of modern family life. A class hierarchy is projected in portrayals of successful, happy families by the media, which uses populist language as a means of concealing the immensely privileged, and often inherited, position of these super-families.

The top of the pile in the Australian media's family hierarchy is still occupied by the British Royal Family. Despite a campaign sponsored by Donald Horne to support republicanism after the dismissal of the Whitlam Government in 1975, such moves have had little success. Anglo-Australian connections are still an important part of the Australian constitutional and legal processes and they are culturally reinforced by the media's consistent devotion to the welfare of British royalty.

However, the media's representation of royal family activities does change significantly over time in relation to the natural ageing processes of the Royals themselves, and depending which Royal Family members are out of favour. In the 1950s the Royal visit to Australia, coming soon after Queen Elizabeth's coronation was the Australian media event of the decade. In the 1980s the Queen and Prince Phillip have become middle-aged figures. The glamour of their position has been passed on to Prince Charles and Lady Di.

The February '83 issue of *Prime Time*, a new Herald and Weekly Times monthly magazine aimed at Australia's ageing population, portrayed the senior Royal couple in this light by showing the Queen happily taking a back seat to the Prince in his role as an expert coachman. The ease and comfort shown in these recent photos, *Prime Time* commented, was indicative of a new mellowness and happiness in the royal couple's relationship. This was a change for the better from earlier public photos which had shown a marked aloofness between them (February '83).

In contrast, Charles and Di have taken over the mantle of youthful Royal glamour. A *Woman's Day* feature about them in February '83 shows pictures of the happy parents and the new baby, accompanying an article by royal biographer Helen Cathcart. The article details the luxuriously secure environment around the royal baby and suggests minor breaks in royal traditions of child-raising. Traditionally the first and second in line to the throne were forbidden from travelling together. But Princess Di had encouraged Charles to fly the three of them to a family gathering at Balmoral last summer.

In an analysis of a 1982 *Women's Weekly* cover featuring Lady Diana and the Queen, John Fiske has argued that Lady Di's image in the Australian media can be critically read as indicating changing perceptions of royalty's place in Australian culture. Fiske emphasises how Di's media image is subliminally associated with Australia, while the Queen is tied to Britain. Strains between the Queen and Lady Di which periodically surfaced over the Princess's public self-presentation are an indication of the re-evaluation of royalty's place in Australia today. Lady Di's youth and informality are contrasted by the *Weekly*, in their cover, with the Queen's ageing formality; the Queen represents the past and Lady Di the future. The result is a re-negotiation of an image of royal femininity which is more in step with contemporary changes in Australian life (Fiske & Copping, October '82).

Subtle reconstructions of the royal image of this kind may be easily overlooked, especially by those of us who find it hard to take the

Australian media's cult of royalty worship seriously. But pro-royalist Australian readers are sensitive to such details. When the Australian media prints more forthright criticism of British royalty they usually do so by reprinting critical British media reports. The *Sun* in January '83, for instance, reprinted a column by British journalist Jean Rook which sharply criticised Lady Di for being rude to reporters at a recent ski-holiday. When in the public eye, Rook claimed, Lady Di had to acknowledge public interest 'because the day that the public's interest in the Royal Family ends, only God can save the lot of them' (*S*, 21 January '83).

As well as linking Australia to British royalty, the commercial media's preoccupation with the aristocracy also connects Australia symbolically with European royalty and Hollywood stardom. The December '82 issue of *New Idea* features a cover story on 'The Year of the Princess' which starred not only Lady Di, but the late Princess Grace of Monaco, her daughter Princess Caroline, and Princesses Anne and Margaret. The article's theme was the role of the Princesses in providing a wealth of emotional experience for their publics.

Despite a few criticisms, Princess Diana was still labelled as the world's favourite. Princess Grace was mourned as an ex-Hollywood great; Princess Caroline was shown emerging from tragedy as a mature, capable woman; Princess Anne was criticised for her indifference to her brother Charles' fatherhood; and Princess Margaret was seen as adopting a suitably low profile in redeeming her mistakes with Roddy Llewelyn—cuttingly described as 'an out of work gardener ... 17 years her junior' (*New Idea*, 25 December '82). Fantasy projections of this kind by the Oz media locate Australia's place in the annals of international royalty, and hold up models of responsible feminine behaviour.

The next step down the ladder in the media hierarchy of happy families belongs to the rich and famous. Robert and Susan Sangster's media visibility is a good example. The focus of attention again is mainly on British elite society, but the Australian connection is that Susan Sangster was formerly the wife of Andrew Peacock.

In a mid-'82 *Daily Telegraph* profile Robert Sangster was described as one of the most amazing racehorse owners in history—a feature likely to kindle interest for many readers. This version of the ideal couple casts him as king of the big spenders with an unprecedented knowledge of horseflesh, while his wife is described as one of the most photographed women in the world. After the break-up with Andrew Peacock Susan Sangster left her children in a Melbourne boarding school, but this is seen as no cause for criticism by the *Telegraph*. The parental responsibilities of the rich, that is, are assessed differently from those of ordinary people (*T*, 15 May '82). The Sangster story has been given new media life through Robert's friendship with Jerry Hall, a California model and some-time girlfriend of Mick Jagger.

Another version of the happy, successful couples story is the marital experience of the cultured and famous. This is an angle more suited to the quality press, and Fairfax's *National Times* profiled the Googie Withers–John McCallum marriage this way in November '82 as 'The Survivors'. Journalist Lucy Wagner referred to their perennial image as the ideal showbiz couple. In an industry where divorce was common, they continued to live and work in complete domestic harmony. The career of Withers and McCallum reads like a 'who's who' in Australian theatrical history, and though they have lived and worked most of their lives in England, the media treats them as surrogate Australians. Other famous cultured couples the media has treated in a similar way are Joan Sutherland and Richard Bonynge and Laurence Olivier and Vivien Leigh (*NT*, 7 November '82).

The marriages of local entertainers and media personalities provide media material which is less socially prestigious but still of public interest. The marriage of Sydney media personalities Clive Robertson and Penny Cook in December '82 sparked off admiring coverage from the *Woman's Day*, the *Daily Telegraph* and other media (*Woman's Day*, 21 December '82, *T*, 6 December '82). Robertson is a well-known radio announcer for the ABC's breakfast show, and in late 1982 he also replaced John Laws on Channel 10's *Beauty and the Beast* show; Cook plays vet Vicky Dean in the high-rating Channel 7 programme *A Country Practice*.

The same edition of the *Woman's Day* also profiled the Sydney Harbour wedding of Cop Shop actress Olga Tamara to Tony Nielsen, a director of Channel 10's *Parkinson in Australia*, as 'Oceans of Love'. A short time later *TV Week* covered the marriage of TV compere Jimmy Hannan's daughter, also married at sea, as 'Melissa's Love Boat' (15 January '83). A few weeks previously Marcia Hines' secret marriage to a Frenchman had attracted after-the-event coverage in the *Mirror* (30 December '82).

The media's romanticism about local and lesser-known celebrities finally reaches a limit. Eventually a kind of anonymous glamour is attached to the marriages of ordinary people. In effect, a space is reserved in the media for the periodic coverage of attractive, but otherwise unremarkable couples who happen to fit the media's needs for filler material, or to act as the basis for seasonal promotions.

Australasian Post, for instance, puts pretty, bikini-clad Jane Robertson on its cover, then features her with boyfriend Jon Lavers in a centre-fold. This centre-fold is not the usual *Playboy* type, but one about potential marital bliss: 'Mr Spunky', as Lavers was crowned by a 1981 fund-raising quest for the multiple sclerosis society, is shown with his girlfriend as an ideal couple. Anonymity reaches its logical conclusion with Baby of the Year contests, as in the Brisbane *Sunday Sun*'s January '83 Sun Summer Baby Contest. Events like this are promotional exercises for the paper, but they reaffirm conventional family relationships and sentimentalise children (9 January '83).

So the Australian media's hierarchy of happy families ranges from royalty to ordinary people, but features royalty, the wealthy and powerful and popular entertainers most prominently. The details of media coverage of family life of this kind are repetitive and prosaic for those readers who have no special interest in the subject, but they are the media's routine way of describing the social context of marriage.

English film critic David Thomson has suggested that the greatest psychological damage done by Hollywood films is not due to their emphasis on violence, but to their preoccupation with romantic love. The same could be said about the Australian commercial media's treatment of the promise of marriage—it is presented as a glossy, sugar-coated pill which conceals an implicit class ordering of everyday social experience. Media coverage of family life tells readers how the social world is constructed and encourages them to expect things to stay that way.

Threats to the Family

Threats to the family are routinely constructed by the media to complement its presentation of happy family news. These threats can be major or trivial, and real or imaginary. Where the good news about happy royal families is chosen from Britain, bad family news is mostly drawn from America. Some local bad family news also becomes so well known—e.g. the Lindy Chamberlain case—that the couples concerned become infamous as well as famous. Women's magazines carry less material of this kind, but the popular metropolitan press and TV habitually use dramatic threats about the family.

Bad family news from overseas supplies the main stories about bizarre and violent crimes against the family. The recurrent theme of these overseas stories is that violent crime, divorce and sexual promiscuity are the worst threats to family life. This emphasis is repeated in the selection and presentation of local family bad news, except that dangers to children's health are also emphasised. In both local and overseas family news there is little routine reporting of domestic violence, divorce is treated superficially, and child abuse is only mentioned occasionally.

Sometimes bad overseas family news concerns British personalities. When tennis-player Chris Evert-Lloyd won the Australian Open in 1982, for instance, the *Telegraph*'s front-page sub-head was 'RUMOURS OVER MARITAL SPLIT MAR VICTORY' (16 December '82). And sometimes bad overseas family news is presented as amusing or startling, as with a Melbourne *Truth* item about Tula, a James Bond girl who'd had a sex change operation and was about to marry.

Bad family news from overseas, however, is more often about tragedies, scandals among celebrities, or about shockingly bizarre American family crimes. The *Sun*'s report of Sean Lennon's memories of his dad, or the *Mirror*'s article on Roxanne Pulitzer's divorce—'SEX SAGA WIFE ROXANNE LEAVES IN DISGRACE' (30 December '82)—are stories of the first and second kind about elite figures. The more regular items about bizarre violent family crimes, however, are about ordinary Americans. Examples here are the *Sun*'s account of the killing of two young children by their nineteen-year-old babysitter in Florida (6 December '82), and the *Mirror*'s copy about a 'SUICIDE DAD'S MURDER TRAIL', a bloody family killing in Toronto, Canada.

Though overseas reports of elite family tragedies are more likely to make the front pages of the Australian popular press, stories about violent crime as a threat to ordinary families gets news priority. Three front pages in the late December–early January period of 82/83 are illustrative. 'ROBBERS SET HOME ABLAZE' was the *Mirror*'s front page, about the robbing and bashing of a Liverpool pensioner in his home by three armed, masked men. 'Home' is, of course, the physical setting for the family. The *Sun* had a first-page story 'CROWD JEERS: ATTACK ON BOY, MOTHER', about the brutal bashing, sexual assault, and robbery which took place on a young Yagoona housewife and son at home (16 December '82). Last, an early '83 *Mirror* piece was 'MOTHER ATTACKED IN LIFT', covering the rape of a woman in a block of flats at Maroubra. Crimes against women here are routinely translated by the media into family language.

A more common type of bad local family news is warnings of danger to children. This is one of the few ways children can get into the metropolitan papers, which otherwise pay little attention to the affairs of childhood. Stories of health threats and accidents are most frequent. 'DEADLY TOYS A THREAT TO THE KIDS' and 'DIET DANGER TO BABIES' are stories from the Brisbane *Sunday Sun* and the Sydney *Sun-Herald* in January '83 (*SS*, 9 January '83; *SH*, 2 January '83) which highlighted environmental and dietary dangers to kids.

There are also routine accident and lost child reports. 'GOD BLESS

THIS HAND', says the *Daily Mirror* about the successful seven hour operation to save a four year old's hand after a domestic accident (16 November '82). More tragically, there are the reports about youths killed in car and motorbike accidents and the effects on their families' lives. On 29 December '82 the *Telegraph* carried a story about how the father of a youth killed with his girlfriend after a high speed chase called on the dead girl's parents to say 'sorry'. This was one of the few times a father was mentioned in bad news stories about kids.

Children are also shown as victims of crime. More rarely, they are shown as guardians of the home themselves, almost like Maoist youth cadres. 'CHARLIES LITTLE ANGELS', went one such *Telegraph* front-page story, about how a group of Chatswood (an affluent Sydney north shore suburb) girls aged between six and ten had watched a local burglary then helped police make an arrest by providing accurate descriptions of the men concerned (22 January '83).

Financial and Medical Media Advice

As well as building up a protective emotional climate around family life in terms of promises of happiness and threats of disaster, the popular commercial media regularly offers advice and counselling about home and family affairs. One level of media advice is financial advice about real estate. The quality as well as the evening press offers regular 'Life and Home' sections where family experiences with home-buying and building are reported. The quality press usually pays more attention to decisions involving major capital outlays, such as home purchase and renovation, where the evening press gives more space to home activities, such as gardening and repairs. Consumer information is also offered by the popular press, as in Helen Wellings' 'Buying Power' column in the *Sun*.

This economic emphasis on home-making activities in the press is supplemented by advertising promotions aimed at the same market. The *Sun*'s section on home design and style by Anne Olsen, for instance, also carries large ads for low-income housing offered by the N.S.W. State Government authority Landcom, as well as for present releases of luxury home units (12 January '83). Men play a very important role in media services of this kind in a range of roles: they act as investment advisors to the general public (Bruce Bond), as practical repairmen (Jim Swartzman's 'Decorator's Hotline' in the *Sun-Herald*), and intermittently are featured in more elite but still home-oriented roles as successful architects or furniture merchandisers (*SMH*, 22 January '83).

Direct attention to the social interactions of family life is also found in the evening press and women's magazines. Especially in the evening press, male authority figures are one of the main sources of family advice. The traditional role of family doctor is still most often filled by men. Dr James Wright is currently the best-known media medico in Australia. As long ago as 1975, however, he was writing in this capacity for the *Woman's Day*; currently he has a time-slot on both the Mike Walsh show and radio 2GB. *New Idea* has a new community health specialist in Dr Michael Smith, while there is also the occasional woman medical expert, as in the *Sun*'s medical report, 'Pulse', with Sue Mahaffies.

Woman's Day uses men as columnists to write about cooking (Peter Russell-Clarke, the egg-man), kid's activities (Keith Smith, ex-kid's radio personality), and entertainment (Andrew Saw), as well as about travel. Men also occupy a prominent place as counsellors in *Prime Time* magazine. There John Message, head of the Human Relations section of the Melbourne Cairnmillar Institute, has a health and living column, along with Dr Ainslie Meares, the Rev. Gordon Powell, and Dr Hugh Sedgwick (February '83).

Women's magazines, however, seem to be using increasingly fewer male authorities in this way, perhaps because of the impact of the women's movement. Men are more prominent in this role in the popular press. Milton Luger, for instance, an 'executive director of the John McGrath foundation' for drug rehabilitation, has a column in the *Telegraph* (31 August '82). Similarly, in the *Sun-Herald*, Dr Lyn Barrows, a psychologist, answers readers' letters about family medical and personal problems. Columns of this kind offer clichéd commonsense advice on family problems. 'Family membership,' writes Barrows, 'invites responsibilities as well as privileges' (*SH*, 20 January '83).

Media Family Counselling

Family counselling and advice is also an increasingly important function of the broadcast media. Advice about the family is given explicitly in some formats, is offered indirectly in the course of some programs, and is implicit in much TV fiction. Generally, TV coverage of the family is positive and optimistic, like its treatment by women's magazines; radio's construction of the family is less glamorous, and its talk shows often reveal serious problems in Australian families.

Partly this is due to different censorship, production, and technical practices used in the two media. As a form, TV suppresses differences, where radio makes more of them: commercial TV is considered 'the' family medium by advertisers, where metropolitan radio is more a collection of divergent voices talking about city life.

Sydney radio programming, considered from the viewpoint of different potential family audiences, gives listeners three main choices. Regular classical and standard music delivered at a slow pace is offered by ABC Radio 1 and 2CH; talk, sports, and some light music, all at a faster rate, are broadcast by 2GB, 2UE, 2KY, and, slower still, by ABC Radio 2; while rapid tempo rock music and machine-gun DJ spiels are provided by 2SM, 2UW, and—more slowly and nostalgically ('Greatest Memories, Latest Hits') by 2WS. Generationally, the first format is for older listeners, the second is for adults, and the third is for kids, teenagers and young adults.

Radio shows offering direct advice to listeners about personal and family problems are mostly carried on Sunday nights, by church-based personalities, such as Father Jim McLaren. Specialist, non-religious advice is also offered to listeners routinely by a range of experts: Dorothy Hall on natural health, Bruce Bond on finance, and Dr James Wright on medical problems.

Many of the conventional talk-shows on Sydney radio in the morning and late evening, however, regularly carry discussions of family issues. There the treatment of these issues is often connected to current politics. 2UE's John Pearce, for instance, asks callers to ring him about the situation of unemployed dads; John Singleton has parents of runaway kids call in to discuss juvenile crime; or Bob Rogers has the families of strikers call up to talk about the effect of strikes on family life (2UE, 8 November '82; 2KY, 25 November '82).

But there are built-in limits to the serious discussion of issues in all commercial talkback formats. No matter how serious the social problem being talked about is, the talkback host will be back at the same time tomorrow with an equally serious problem to keep talking about. There is a routinisation of experience which defuses serious subject matter.

The dominance of men in talking about family issues is also a limiting factor. Interpersonal communication research shows that men interrupt women in normal speech interaction more than vice-versa. Women on Sydney non-commercial radio like Margaret Throsby often encourage public discussion of issues by bringing together experts and activists in social affairs, and positively mediating between them— which is what 'media' is supposed to mean. But some of the long-winded monologues delivered by commercial talk-show hosts like John

Pearce and John Tingle repress communication instead of encouraging it.

Most of the men who act as talkback comperes are also established media personalities, and middle-aged family men in their own right. They are predisposed to favor conventional solutions to family problems which arise in on-air discussion. This is so even with younger, more liberal talkback men like 2UE's Ian Parry-Okeden. Writing in his *Mirror* column 'My Word' in September '82, he discussed teenage morals based on his accidental meeting with a young girl who was an old family friend. Aged 13 she was waiting at a bus-stop, smoking pot, and necking with teenage boys.

Parry-Okeden wondered how parents of teenagers today coped with their children's involvement with peers, sex, drugs, rock 'n' roll, and television. His column ended by citing two current Top 40 songs"I Know What Boys Like', and 'Goody Two Shoes'—as examples of destructive social values (13 September '82). The limitation on this kind of conventional media moralism is that it perceives the promotion of aggressive behaviour by the media, but cannot explicitly identify its sources, as the commentator is part of the commercial media himself.

Counselling and advice on TV is more indirect. There is no immediate viewer involvement in TV as in radio, though this could change with cable TV. Television still uses personal family problems as a source of entertainment in shows like *Beauty and the Beast*, which would not exist unless viewers were gullible enough to write in about their problems. More importantly, family life is the basis for those Australian TV serials now called soaps.

Soaps should be something that Australian TV could do very well. There is a tradition of family serials in Australian radio and novel production, going back to *Blue Hills*, *Bellbird*, *Dr Paul*, and *When a Girl Marries*. However the only clear critical success so far has been *The Sullivans*, which was more of a historical serial than a soap. As with recent Australian films, TV finds it hard to deal with contemporary life, even as fiction. Shows like *A Country Practice* and *Sons and Daughters* are often stilted and unconvincing, and seem as likely to vanish in the ratings as did *Taurus Rising*, *Arcade*, and *Skyways*.

Family Advertising

The other dimension of television which has specific effects on family life is advertising. Few studies have yet been made of the cumulative picture of family life that TV advertising conveys. Generally, family associations seem less important in product promotions than attachment of the product to a youthful peer group, or to prominent sports or entertainment personalities. What is well-researched, however, is that a good deal of the content of advertising directed specifically to children aims at selling junk food.

A number of groups have been pressuring the Australian government to take action about this for years. In a May 1980 submission to the Nutrition Standing Committee of the National Health and Medical Research Council, the Australian Consumers' Association had identified many health problems in the Australian population as being linked with an extremely high per capita level of sugar intake. Sugar, of course, is one of the ingredients in alcohol, particularly beer. In its later 1981 survey of Sydney TV advertising ACA found that food ads were 32 per cent of all TV ads broadcast in one week, and that drinks, especially alcohol, received the most promotion of all foods. Of all food advertised on television in that week, ACA concluded that only 20 per cent of advertised varieties made a positive contribution to nutritional health.

The promotion of alcohol on TV is allowed after 7.30 pm, though audience research shows that the eldest child under thirteen in many families continues to watch until 8.30, and that AO programmes are not allowed to be shown before 8.30 pm. In this time-slot TV advertising is literally soaked with alcohol advertising. ACA drew attention to the recurrent use of well-known sporting and media personalities to sell alcohol. It found figures such as John Newcombe, who had been prominently associated with patriotic pro-Australia campaigns, as well as pro-Liberal election commercials, endorsing alcohol in this way.

The concern of media researchers with TV's effects on children traditionally has looked at the effects of violent screen behaviour. But the clearest case that TV is damaging to children, however, can be made in terms of the use of TV advertising to sell sugar-rich food to children, and alcohol and tobacco to adults, with sugar-dependency bridging the gap. Real Australian family violence is sparked off by alcohol. TV advertising which pressures young children into sugar-rich diets, and glamorises drinking for adolescents via images of tough football heroes and lifesavers, encourages young Australian boys to grow up into pot-bellied, drunken, violent men.

The slotting of commercials in particular programmes and against each other is the way that TV programmers use to make subliminal associations for their audiences. Before its cancellation in late '82, the John Laws show *The Reporters* made use of the heavy repetition of beer commercials. Quite dissimilar products can be symbolically associated to make them more attractive together than separately.

Quick-Eze, the State Bank, and Great Western Champagne have nothing in common, but routine television fantasy turns them into a consecutive set of ads which change Quick-Eze into a World War II air briefing session, link the State Bank with a dream cartoon home, and show Ken Rosewall enjoying Great Western bubbly. Advertisements for indigestion relief, banking services, and champagne, become transmogrified into glamorisations of militarism, domesticity, and alcoholism.

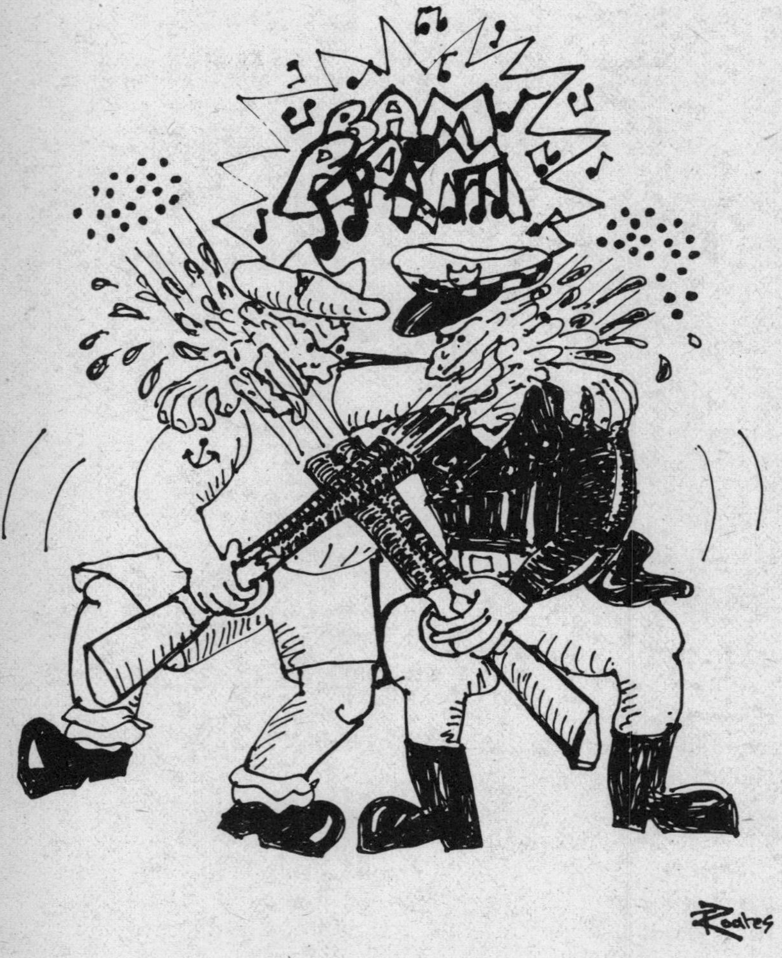
BAM
BAM

CHANNEL 3

10 Starmen—Oz Rock 'n' Role Survival Fantasies

Rock is pure fantasy.
Ozrock is pure shit. That is, it's great.
But, how come a supposedly non-violent country produces such aggro rock music?
For some fantastic suggestions now read on.

Track 1/ Down in Hollywood

One of the legends Australian travellers spread about the States is that Americans automatically like Australians. They don't. Most Americans don't know anything about Australia.

My first night in the States a few years ago—where else but Hollywood?—I met an American Ozrockophile. Harvey was a mildly sad case. His room was wreathed with posters of Olivia Newton-John, whom he'd met once and fantasised about ever since. He'd worked as a roadie for Air Supply, had all the LRB tapes, and had been to Oz briefly on R&R during Vietnam.

Harvey worked in a big second-hand book store on Hollywood Boulevard. Sometimes I'd catch him rapping with a few pals late at night on the sidewalk as the kids skated past with their boom-boxes. Harvey was Japanese-American from Hawaii, and didn't care much for LA. His dream was to live in the lucky country and marry a nice girl from Melbourne. Too many queers in Sydney, he said.

For him, Ozrock was middle-of-the-road plastic. The bland international sound of Air Supply, Olivia Newton-John, the Bee Gees, and Rick Springfield. Yet recently, Air Supply's lead singer said Oz was really a rock'n roll country.

Originally published in *Island Magazine*, June 1982.

Track 2/ Too Old to Rock'n Roll

So how did the fifties bodgies become eighties Kingswood dads?

The tension between rage and respectability in Ozrock goes back to Johnny O'Keefe and Col Joyless. Col was always a cleancut young lad who had an elective affinity with the equally spotless Hendo. In 1962 Col was described in *TV Week* as the same nice guy that everyone knows in public. Quote: 'Col is 25 and lives with his mother. His sports are water-skiing and collecting guns' ... (?)

Even JO'K was whitewashed after a while. Liberty records re-labelled him 'The Boomerang Boy' and faithlessly promised he'd be among the top American stars in six months. Johnny B. Goode. 'Nine out of ten bodgies are decent,' said John.

The first wave of Ozrock stars who started out rough and ready were all soon desanitised and deodorised. In 1959 Johnny Rebb was voted one of the best dressed men on TV. The trick, he revealed, was to wear nothing loud. Later Johnny Devlin confessed to once being a teenage hood. But by then he'd moved to North Ryde and was happily married.

Track 3/ Back in Black

AC/DC, Midnight Oil, Rose Tattoo, some Cold Chisel and some Men at Work ... That's rock which isn't watered down. Ozrock does violence best. *Mad Max* and *Chant of Jimmie Blacksmith* do the same. Australians aren't non-violent. They're personally tough and aggressive. Their apathy to politics and culture comes out of scepticism and distrust. Australians are the rejects of British culture who haven't decided to become Americans. Australians are rock 'n' role survivors.

Oz culture produces great heavy rock groups because of the suppressed current of nervous violence that's in much Australian daily life. And it produces groups rather than individual stars. The few who go solo usually fade away. Remember Darryl Braithwaite, Shirley Strachan or Marc Hunter? Australians perform well in sports, but don't have a vital enough performance musical tradition to produce solo rock stars. Or actors. Can you imagine Malcolm Fraser in the movies?

Ozrock rarely explores personal or sexual ambiguity. There are no David Bowies or Lou Reeds in Ozrock, except maybe for Peter Allen, who's a cabaret singer. And there are no gay rock stars in the all-male scene. Lesbian-feminist bands like the Stray Dags play to local Sydney pub and dance crowds. Ozrock audiences are sharply divided in their musical tastes. Abba and the Village People pulled big crowds here, but the teeny-bopper and gay market they play for is mainstream bland.

Commercial Break One

DJ   'Count the Notes Fred—here we go.'
(SOUND FX) Splotch, splotch, splotch, etc.

DJ   'How many notes Fred?'

Fred   'Forty-three.'

DJ   'Tough luck Fred. Forty four. Never mind—you've won our $60 000 lottery ticket instead, and, on what station Fred?'

Fred   'Shit.'

DJ   'Fred? Fred? Yes, that's it—the new poo UW. Right! You poo, we all poo too. Now back to more musik!'

Track 4/ At Home He Feels Like a Tourist

Edward Carpenter, a friend of McLuhan's, did anthropological work in New Guinea in the late sixties. He predicted then that radio would have a shattering effect on tribal life. No one seems to have bothered to check up, though the Phantom—a fifties comic book hero—became a popular local figure and was used in some government campaigns to attract attention.

Carpenter's claim recalls the Victorian experience of tribal people's reaction to white culture generally, and the camera in particular. They thought it would steal their souls. This isn't so far different from what seems to have happened with American media culture and its international audiences. There has been a mass invasion of public inner space by American media culture. The U.S. media report the activities of a number of world leaders and celebrities while keeping the majority locked into the dream machine as passive audiences. Attention means money. The ratings are power. May McNair-Anderson be with you.

TV locks people into a double-bind of object consumption and emotional constipation. It concentrates on the nuclear family, defining it by the number of goodies each little unit saves up. The state is projected as a nuclear family compact. The giant corporation is the (typically absent) father, the mother—a nervous, nagging mum—is the national government. Their children are the whole celebrity system—the rock stars, the World Series Cricket yobbos, political hotshots, the jetset, etc. And, as in *Being There*—the Koszinski/Sellers novel-film—there is no difference anymore between real leaders and fantasy leaders, though they're usually American. This is dissociation. TV is making a cryogenic society. Media is the embalming fluid the culture is shooting up to keep itself going.

Although this constant circulation of celebrities by the media is explained 'rationally' as profits, communication, entertainment, and so on, it's not rational. The TV world is under control and the real world isn't. It's out of control. People watch TV knowing or fearing this, and watch TV to forget it. So the underlying concern of the mass audience with media celebrity is probably more a deeply repressed obsession with death. Celebrity worship is the modern world's respectable form of death worship. Death isn't welcome in politely sanitised urban life, so it becomes the staple subject matter of media entertainment.

Finally the masses turn on their own stars like cannibals. Elvis and Errol are shown to have been degenerates, Marilyn was a nympho, Bing was mean, etc. When celebrities die or misbehave their reputation can be spat on and kicked. Nathanael West's *Day of the Locust* is the best fictional example I know of that deep pool of resentment underlying the public's admiration. At the end of the novel a faceless mid-west crowd of fans riot during a Hollywood premiere.

The same vomited-up resentment was thrown at the idiot rich on stage at 2SM's fabulous Opera House concert of 1979. Let them eat rock, said Jon English: for his performance he got to sing Waltzing Matilda in the next VFL final.

Track 5/ Where Women Glow and Men Plunder

Rock 'n' role careers are the astrological death charts for all celebrities. Morrison dead, Hendrix, Bon Scott, Alex Harvey, etc. all dead. Rock is the music of the time and the times are violent. Rock is the production line, jets, semi-trailers, and now the computer. The guitar is dead, long live the Moog.

Rock is overstimulation. It dramatises the rhythm of city life. It's mostly a nighttime music, talking of good times, pleasure, booze, dope, and sex. Sex & drugs & rock 'n' role. But rather than being an alternative formula for a new lifestyle (not just a group, but a way of life, as old Stones PR went), rock as a business is used to support the status quo.

Fantastic plastic 2SM does it by pounding out its rock formula six and a half days a week, and playing church muzak on the remaining half Sunday. 2SM is a Catholic radio station. Rock on 2SM is not just played, it is programmed. It is designed to wrap harmlessly round the listeners, routinising their listening patterns so the commercials can be slipped in subliminally. Top-ten songs are recycled quickly as pimple commercials. Ian Drury's hymn of praise 'Spasticus' is turned into pimple cream commercials, which usually are spoken in American.

Jay-jay-jay, G-G-George here ... George is great 2SM/MMM material but is still serving his apprenticeship with Auntie. Sit on it George. 2JJJ is okay sometimes. It's much more subversive and anti-commercial than 2SM but it's as anti-intellectual, and it publicises government welfare activities uncritically.

Commercial Break Two

'This week only at the Stadium Negara in KL, be sure to catch the repeat charity show of Anita Sarawak.

'Ignore last week's *New Thrill* report that the average jeans and T-shirt clad youngster walked out of the stadium after the show feeling anything but ... satisfied.

'The night will not be without fun. Since her marriage to Marantike Abdullah, she rocks, prances about the stage, she wriggles, she rolls—for one and a half hours non-stop.

'And this time she will sing Rock Around the Clock!'

(Lee Kuan Yew banned rock and long hair from Singapore because it made the busy Singaporeans less predictable.)

Track 6/ Let the Good Times Roll

The effect of celebrity worship on personality cuts two ways. It collapses the divisions between fantasy and reality in public life, turning world politics into a giant TV game show with the Reds and the Feds as baddies and goodies. Charlton Heston joins Malcolm Fraser and Ronald Reagan in bringing you the Polish Solidarity Special.

Superstars existed before World War II, but then they were just film stars whose glamour depended on their detachment from the ordinary world. The modern media celebrity is more all-pervasive. Famous people today may or may not have done something special. Warhol's celebrity law now reads: every white middle-class American will be famous for five minutes in the future.

Celebrity worship also shapes people's self-image. They either consciously reject the model, as do many working-class Australians, and distance the media from their own lifestyles, or partly embrace it, which is more a middle-class solution. Conscious rejection of the media world, however, does nothing to prevent the media taking over traditional working-class activities, as with TV sport. It also ignores the political effects of media values. Singleton continues to be accepted at Labor-owned station 2KY, despite his own right-wing politics.

The other alternative is to partly accept the celebrity system. Socially, the outcome here is for more fashion-conscious groups to separate themselves from others to cultivate their differences. Interpersonally, there is a heightened sense of distrust between people, and increased self-abuse (emotional, instead of physical masturbation), and a gradual devolution of intimacy between people. You're a cruiser or a loser.

The result can be growth and self-experimentation via identification with media role models, or it can be herpes, drug or drink dependence, breakdown, suicide, or conversion to Rajneesh or Hare Krishna. Out of all this come the survivors. Rock 'n' role survival is just the tip of a mountain range of icebergs about personal and social survival today.

Track 7/ Are We Not Men? We Are Devo

Someone's knockin' at my door—who can it be now? My chance to go on Cash Capsule? Great! Do I have to reveal my real identity?

Barry Crocker has his arm round Tommy Hanlon. Tommy's talking about his Mum and Toowoomba. My Mum lived in Toowoomba too, and I was born in Tenterfield like Peter Allen. So how come when he does a singing commercial where I work for $10 000 I'm here watching TV in black and white.

Will Ozrock survive? Will Australia become part of America? Will Molly marry Jon?

Who cares. Let the good times roll.

11 Militarism in the Australian Media

Since the election of Ronald Reagan as President of the United States, the threat of renewed international conflict has seen themes of violence and conflict heightened in the Australian media. The attempted presidential assassination, the Russian threat to Poland, continuing violence in Northern Ireland, and the Peacock–Fraser leadership dispute have all fuelled the media's pre-occupation with social conflict in the last few months.

Admittedly, a style of tough, socially divisive journalism is nothing new for Australia; *The Bulletin* in the 1980s and *Smith's Weekly* in the 1940s epitomised Australian yellow journalism, and were popular, nationalistic, and often vicious. This is the same style which Rupert Murdoch's popular papers still employ. What has changed in international journalism since then, however, is that the primacy of the quality press has been further reduced by its incorporation into wider non-newspaper corporate structures, the effects of TV, and by increasing cross-ownership between quality and popular newspapers, especially in Australia.

In what follows the Murdoch organisation's influence on the style of current Australian journalism will be explored as a way of analysing media-generated violence. So far the discussion of media violence has been mainly restricted to children's TV, but by examining the role of the Murdoch group as a national trend-setter it can be argued that their style of aggressive journalism has set the current tone for Australian news reporting generally. This has actively discouraged the development of more socially responsive media: the Australian media leaders now set chauvinist standards and styles which are reproduced by their followers in the industry.

Originally published in *Australian Quarterly*, Spring, 1981.

Gutter Journalism vs the New Journalism

Despite Professor Henry Mayer's warning against a critical preoccupation with such highly visible media magnates, and despite Mr Murdoch's pre-eminence in the Australian scene, there is a curious lack of information about the extent of his real cultural influence. In a sense he simply is his media: he is the *New York Post*, the *Daily Mirror*, and *The Australian*, and his media editors and executives are approved extensions of the Murdoch persona. More important, however, is his success in developing a distinctively Australian style of aggressive journalism. Rough and tumble journalism is not uniquely Australian, but Murdoch is the first to succeed in applying the Australian version of the product to the American and English markets. What I want to consider here is not the Murdoch group's own role, but its influence in setting the pace for Australian journalism more broadly.

Although the techniques of scurrilous Australian journalism seem to have transplanted successfully to the U.S. via the *Post*, the exchange process hasn't worked both ways. Lacking a comparable framework of media freedom and diversity, neither Australian print nor broadcast journalism has developed much sophistication about its own processes. There has been little of the American 'new journalism' in Australia so far, and now the new journalism has waned in the U.S.A. During the last year of Jimmy Carter's presidency the Iranian issue focused American journalism on the prospects of war and violence. After the disillusioned isolationism of the post-Vietnam, post-Nixon era, a new sense of national bellicosity seems to have developed in American politics, and the media have played a leading role in fuelling this aggressiveness. The new chauvinism comes out in different ways in Australia, but it is still consistently anti-communist, anti-Soviet, pro-English, and pro-American.

Channel Nine's award winning news programme *60 Minutes* probably has been the best local adaptation of an American new journalism formula so far to Australia TV. Erik Barnouw has pointed to the limitations of the original CBS format—the use of superstar reporters, an avoidance of complexity, the limited use of non-network documentary footage, the programme's fictional overtones—yet it deservedly remains one of the more respected American weekly TV news programmes.

Similar criticisms can be made of the Australian version, but compared with the rather stale formulas of older TV news formats, *60 Minutes* is sometimes a fine programme.

Perhaps radio has been the best performer. Some commercial broadcasters such as Brian White, Steve Raymond and Derryn Hinch have created formats where they can state their own opinions freely as part of their radio reporting, but mostly the impulse of the new journalism seems to have dissipated in the more cynical and anti-intellectual Australian context. Some notable dead-ends in radio here would have to include the obscurity of much feminist and educational broadcasting, the radical chic 2JJJ style, and worst of all the buffoonery of the Laws–Singleton–Pearce style talk shows.

The record of the new Australian journalism in print is no better. It helped in sparking off small journals such as *Nation Review* and the *New Journalist*, but so far has not had a positive influence on mainstream Australian journalism. Rather it seems to have made local journalism more aggressive and divisive than usual. It has become more of a journalism of revenge, which constantly appeals to a sense of latent public resentment and acts as an inducement to conflict. Public resentment is kept aroused by regular provocative reports on a diverse range of current affairs—strikes, unemployment, homosexuality, crime, the prison system, and so on. These reports are normally presented in the framework of a simplistically personalised adversary system which encourages readers to think simple personal solutions are possible. Currently the media's reproduction of patterns of social divisiveness is being complemented by a government sponsored advertising campaign which stresses national unity (*SMH*, 21 March '81).

American Influences on Australian TV News

The unstated assumption of this argument so far is that Australian media today are being increasingly influenced by American practices. Although as yet the question of American influence on Australian TV news has attracted less attention than the issue of American dominance in the supply of entertainment programmes to Australian networks, it seems no less important. Historically Australian print journalism has existed for a much longer period than broadcasting and mostly has been modelled along English lines. Australian radio broadcasting, however, was established one hundred years later in the 1920s and bore closer resemblance to American commercial organisations. Further, the introduction of television to postwar Australia coincided with a high point in Australian–American political and economic contact.

Specific examples of American influence on Australian TV news can be found in programmes on all major channels. Channel 0/10's introduction of *Eyewitness News* was modelled directly on an American format. Similarly Gerald Stone, the producer of Channel 9's *60 Minutes*, is originally an American whose experience in TV journalism in both Australia and the U.S. facilitated the transfer of the show to Australian conditions. The late Bob Moore of Channel 2's now defunct *Monday Conference* also had studied American broadcast journalism with Fred Friendly in the U.S.

Lastly, the image of Channel 9's principal newsreader, Brian Henderson, seems to have been influenced by the public image of Walter Cronkite. In American CBS new programmes Cronkite rates consistently high as a credible news reporter and commentator, and the theme of Channel 9's promotional campaign for Henderson over the last few years has been the 'Brian told me' approach which stresses his familiarity and credibility. At least in this case, however, Australians seem to have bought the American news package without the content. Cronkite was an experienced print journalist who had covered the Normandy invasion during World War II. By contrast, Brian Henderson's earlier Australian TV role was to be compere of *Bandstand*, a 1960s rock 'n' roll show which was modelled on the lines of Dick Clark's American show of the same name.

During the second half of the 1970s the increasing dominance of American style news formats was reinforced by national political circumstances and by technological change. Politically, since 1975 the Fraser Government has limited the effectiveness of ABC broadcasting by its severe budgetary constraints. The ABC's recurrent—and still unsolved—dilemma has been whether to model itself on commercial lines and chase the ratings, or to concentrate on quality broadcasting for a minority audience. This period of stringency and indecision has created a negative climate which has not favoured much experimentation in developing new news or current affairs formats. The clearest sign of the ABC's weakness in this area has been the regular loss of nationally-known staff to the commercials. Mike Willesee, George Negus and now Ross Symonds have all followed that career path, which rarely seems to lead in the opposite direction.

Technologically, international changes in the television and telecommunications markets also have fostered American rather than English influence on Australian TV. Satellite relay has proved to be an indispensable part of international news and sports reporting and American space technology leads the world in this regard. Similarly, the current proposal for the introduction of cable TV to Australia is based largely on American and Canadian precedents, not English.

Cable and satellite technologies have now been interfaced in the U.S. to produce the first all-news cable services. The future development of specialist TV news broadcasting, that is, is firmly in the hands of American TV producers.

Two further comments on Australian–American differences in the context of TV news are relevant. First, American media in the 1970s have gradually adopted federal employment policies favouring affirmative action for minority groups. In effect this has dramatically increased the visibility of women in American TV news broadcasts. There has as yet been no Australian equivalent. Second, it is arguable that standards of excellence in news reporting should be decided chiefly in terms of their national origins. Ideally Australians should take the best of American and English news reporting practices and develop them for their own purposes, rather than patriotically emulate the BBC or profitably copy CBS. Let us now return to the theme of violence in Australian TV news by looking in more detail at the roles played by Australian TV news teams and newsmen.

The Image of Australian TV Newsmen

In broadcast TV the danger of a chauvinist style of journalism colouring news reporting is much greater than in print journalism, as the medium requires more drastic simplification of issues. Here the media actors who most visibly personify the values of the new journalism today—in Australia or overseas—are the TV news journalists. The successful TV news image internationally is that of a person who is part 'Mr Average' and part 'Mr TV Star'. A sense of glamour is always there, though usually it is understood and takes second place to the projection of an image of reliability and ordinariness.

The second primary quality TV newspeople have is that they are unmistakably members of a team. This is usually a male-dominated team which often behaves with a sports-oriented competitive ethos. Members of the team project a sense of solidarity among themselves, while team animosity is selectively directed at outsiders who do not fit the parameters of TV news values. Lastly, TV news teams project their own personalities squarely into the interpretation of events. Australian TV news personalities tend to present themselves as tough, smart, or cute. Willesee is tough first and smart second; Richard Carleton is smart and sometimes tough; while Katrina Lee, Roger Climpson, Brian Henderson, Ross Symonds and James Dibble are cute.

Low-key glamour, team membership and qualified individualism are the basic parts of a plausible TV news image. Additionally Australian news presenters tend to be political jocks: there are very few women involved in Australian TV news reporting. Where there are, as with Katrina Lee or Caroline Jones, they are often involved in reporting 'women's issues'. Both Lee and, to a lesser extent, Jones project a softer note of maternal solicitude into the harsh world of public affairs reporting, which is how women are expected to behave traditionally.

The TV newsman image also is normally interpreted as an adversary masculine role. The most frequent mode of personal interaction tends to be a two or three person confrontation; wider audiences are rarely used in Australian news shows. Generally, the TV newsman acts more as a provocative referee than as a non-partisan intermediary. Here the behavioural image of TV newsmen is drawn more from sporting contests and tough investigative journalism than from alternative positive models of interpersonal discussion. Newsmen's roles are similarly distorted in the U.S. and England, but not as drastically; Australian culture is more aggressively masculine than either, so the norms of desirable masculine behaviour weigh more heavily on Australian TV news journalists. Their model of intelligent macho behaviour is the other side of the coin of the bland, cute newsreaders at family newstime.

Militarism on Nationwide

As an example of how the Australian media currently perpetuate violence, one episode of the ABC's programme *Nationwide* will be examined. This is a news analysis programme shown week nights at 9.30 following the national news. The particular episode discussed here was shown the night before the attempted assassination of Ronald Reagan. My claim is that the programme's tone was consistently alarmist and socially divisive. The show reinforced a current national state of anxiety about overseas enemies and internal fifth-columnists. In the same week both the *National Times* and *The Bulletin*, Australia's only national weekly newspaper and news magazine, both featured alarmist anti-Russian stories (*NT*, 29 March '81; *B*, 31 March '81).

There were four items on *Nationwide*: a report on the Bogle–Chandler case; an interview with the Polish Ambassador to Australia; a discussion of the erosion of civil liberties via compulsory metric conversion; and an interview about the then controversial new teaching kit on homosexuality for N.S.W. schools. The common theme of all these items was an ostensible concern for the loss of liberties, however this theme progressively was displaced into an encitement to see the Russians and N.S.W. homosexuals as ready to ravish both Poland and Australia. Themes of espionage, high intrigue, and potential danger were used to stimulate a conservative political reaction.

Three of the show's four items were treated seriously while one was handled as light relief. TV news programmes are constructed to flow in a similarly compelling way as commercials and soap operas; they resemble soaps more in their duration, but their internal structure is closer to a commercial. Normally there is only one key message in a programme, which is presented in a direct stimulus–response manner. In the first segment the audience's attention was captured with scandal and intrigue. The second spot introduced the real element of danger—the Russians. The third segment was comic-relief. Lastly came the reinforcement for the previous anti-Russian message, except this time the finger was pointed at N.S.W. homosexuals.

The opening established an anxiety-ridden climate. *Nationwide*'s Paul Murphy quizzed Chandler about his wife's mysterious death years earlier. He responded by explaining that Murdoch's paper the *Mirror* had re-opened the issue by deciding to do a feature series on the crime, whether he co-operated or not. Because TV news personalises issues as a means of simplifying them, it is necessary here to comment critically on the dominant personal images projected in the show. In this light Chandler came across in a mildly heart-rending way as 'Mr Victim'. The drama mounted with his claim that the KGB and CIA were involved, and that he had asked for one million dollars compensation from the Australian government to re-open the case.

Nationwide then went straight to the key item with Richard Carleton's Canberra interview with the Polish ambassador. In contrast to Chandler—who was presented as a rather shadowy victim figure—the Polish ambassador was 'Mr Tough', who circumspectly discussed the details of the confrontation. Carleton, as the programme's heavyweight interviewer, kept probing unsuccessfully for controversial comment on the Russian threat. The segment finished with the two men getting into a near-hysterical *Casablanca* routine about the prospects of Russian invasion. Then came the light relief.

This was an interview with Stephen Murray-Smith, editor of *Overland* and a well-known Melbourne academic, discussing the compulsory features of metric conversion. In the context of the Russian–Polish confrontation this item had a rather bathetic quality and presented Murray-Smith as 'Mr Silly'. This part of the show was the only one to be compered by a woman. Though Murray-Smith came across as genuinely earnest about his case, the item was trivialised by provoking the anti-academic and anti-intellectual predispositions of the Australian public. As in the U.S. (and probably to a much greater degree) the Australian media consistently caricature teachers and educationalists while at the same time using them as a source of cheap expertise. In the context of this particular programme the producers were introducing a note of tension relief before introducing the next piece of chauvinistic material.

The episode concluded with Paul Murphy discussing a controversial sex education teaching kit for N.S.W. schools with Eddie Ashmore, one of the kit's producers. The Federal Minister for Education had already publicly disapproved of the kit and tried to remove funding because of the project's focus on homosexuality. Here the spectre of an invasion was again being raised, except this time it was homosexuals who were claimed to be the threat. Mr Ashmore, who stated that the material was not meant to approve or condone its subject matter, was presented as 'Mr Serious', and therefore as a role model for all serious people worried about the condition of the world.

Conclusion: The Sources of Media Violence

Programmes like this play a central part in orchestrating many of the events they report. Here the first two interview subjects explicitly criticised the role of the media in aggravating the issue, the third subject was initiated directly by *Nationwide*, while media omission and distortion also played a part in subsequent public discussion of the teaching kit issue. As well as the prior involvement of TV news programmes in the definition of many of the events they report, such formats use the normal processes of simplification which TV journalists are obliged to use. To adapt Bernstein's socio-linguistic terms to a media context, TV producers and journalists use an elaborated visual code, which most of the audience—who have either restricted or elaborated print codes—cannot follow in depth. That TV news has little recall value may be due as much to the patterns of systematic distortion employed in TV news language, as to its trivial content.

In short, the programme focused on current Australian alarm about potential Russian intervention in Poland in such a way as to aggravate tension and foster social division. A pro-militarist news policy of this kind serves as a means of reproducing domestic violence by provoking antagonism towards vulnerable, unpopular minority groups. This is not meant as a claim that ABC journalism has fallen directly under the sway of the Murdoch organisation in any conspiratorial sense. Rather, ABC TV news journalism today has sunk to an extremely low standard in the wake of the Fraser government's sustained restrictions on the organisation. Murdoch's rough-and-tumble style of journalism has set the current model of Australian news reporting and groups like the ABC are dragged along in producing chauvinistic reports.

However, the long-term sources of this reproduction of violence through the media are not uniquely Australian. They stem from the power struggles that exist in and between media monopolies themselves, from their subordination to the wider economic system, through advertising and from the scale of male dominance in their organisational structures. These private corporate tensions are expressed publicly through a series of destructive media fantasies about sex, crime, violence, and war, which are as compulsively expressed as any Soviet propaganda themes. When the media function constructively they perform a culturally stabilising role, but when they malfunction they reproduce destructive patterns of violence and militarism. Militarism is directed at external enemies, while patterns of social divisiveness are projected internally at weak minority groups who are publicly fantasised about as the enemy within.

In August 1981, President Reagan had just announced the U.S.'s development of the neutron bomb. In the same week the ABC's much-publicised new science programme *Towards 2000* went to air, with one of the segments treating the American Cruise missile as an a-political scientific marvel. The media's contributions to social violence, that is, are dynamic and on-going, and studies of their effects cannot realistically be restricted to media reports at any one time.

12 Men At Work

Work is the key to men's public identity in industrial societies. It's the most important activity in the lives of most Australian men. What men do with their leisure time—playing sport, gambling, drinking, or driving—is also central to how men define themselves socially, but the way they spend their leisure will usually depend on the nature of their work.

Every industrial culture—Russian as well as American—rates work as the most important male activity. Yet there are notable intercultural differences in the ways work is seen and socially organised. Aboriginals, for instance, never accepted the white Australians' attitudes to work or family life, and consequently find themselves pushed to the edge of society. The ethnic groups who came to Australia after the war also had different cultural values to work from British-Australians.

Presently there is as much disagreement about how work should be re-organised in Australia as there is about the future of the family. Most national discussions of work, however, talk about it in material terms, taking the factor of personal identity for granted. My concern in this chapter is more to consider how men's work defines their public identity and private self-image.

People and Work Today

At a 1981 Australian Institute of Political Science summer school about the future of work, Paul Barton, a visiting American government official, was the only speaker to address the issue of work and identity directly. Characteristically, the contributions by Australians were made by economists, welfare workers, politicians, and managers. Barton made two main points—work had become even more important to people as a means of self-respect and self-identification, and that this was due in part to the erosion of wider social roles in the family, church and community (Wilkes, 57). At a time of rapid social change and economic recession, that is, people's work becomes one of the main things they hold onto as a source of personal identity and financial security.

Increased expectations about jobs, however, are no automatic guarantee of job satisfaction, just as greater expectations about marriage are no guarantee of happiness. A national study in 1973 made by Fred Emery suggested that though the majority of Australians were satisfied with their jobs, this was more a sense of relative satisfaction. While approximately half of the people surveyed were satisfied with their jobs, one-third were indifferent, and the remainder were hostile to work. Since then the threat of unemployment has increased dramatically. As Victorian Labor MP Barry Jones has commented, the social distance between people with jobs and those without is like 'a raft at sea with a great number of sharks around . . . you are either on the raft and alright or off the raft . . . in utter disaster' (Wilkes, 137). There is now a sense of absolute desperation that people must work.

The most important factor Emery identified as making a job a good one was the element of autonomy or elbow-room involved. Other related factors were chances of promotion, learning on the job, and financial rewards. Those most sensitive to quality-of-work issues were younger, better educated, with higher status jobs. The likelihood of apathy to work-quality increased with age. Apathy to work also increases with people's distance down the social scale. Emery's survey showed that the 10 per cent of respondents who'd given up on both work and life were mainly foreign-born, unskilled, and poorly educated. More than two-thirds of working migrant women were identified as disadvantaged, while he found the most job dissatisfaction among workers in the transport and manufacturing industries (Emery, 58).

How work pressures are felt among disadvantaged workers depends on their sex and age. Working women experienced some pressures in their thirties, a time when their children had reached adolescence, and work pressures peaked in their forties—a time coinciding with menopause. Work pressure then declined rapidly on women after age 46. For men, the peak pressures mainly came at the pre-retirement age, from 50 onwards, but another acute period of job dissatisfaction was experienced by men between the ages of 36–46, the time of their male mid-life crisis.

These figures are now dated, and some of Emery's cultural explanations of their causes are open to dispute, but his survey still clearly indicates how the sexes experience different pressure points at different stages of their working lives. Because of the biological and cultural demands of child-raising, women usually leave the workforce at an earlier period in their careers than men, and they subsequently experience different pressures when they re-enter the job. Men, on the other hand, are more consistently committed to working continuously through their lives. Some men also work in much harder, more dangerous and dirty jobs. So when men finally do stop working, for some there is a loss of identity amounting to a loss of will to live. Immediate post-retirement deaths are far more common for men than women.

Women's emotional commitments are not so singly centred on one role. Emery found the greatest period of unhappiness for men at work was between 46 and 55. Thirteen per cent of his sample in that age group saw life as boring, miserable, lonely or empty. Though men over 55 had more personal happiness, they had less hope about the future. Women scored better on expectations of both hope and happiness than men of the same age, despite—or because of?—their being in jobs which were usually of lower quality.

The way unhappy older men and disadvantaged workers cope with job dissatisfaction is by withdrawal—both on and off the job. Dissatisfied workers on the job behaved as loners, showing what Emery labelled 'the dumb ox syndrome'—'I just do what I have to do and don't get involved with other people while on the job'. Off the job, disadvantaged workers took longer to recover from work, though their jobs were not so much physically or mentally demanding as demeaning. They also had less energy left over to involve themselves socially with others or in community activities.

Technical Men: Work as Social Engineering

In evaluating contemporary arguments about work, technology, and industrial conflict, it is essential to understand the social impact of the postwar communications revolution. There is as yet little clear historical perspective about this. Australian government and union policies about technology only began to change quickly in the late seventies. Changes in Western society between 1940 and 1970, however, have been as momentous in re-organising society as were the first thirty years of the industrial revolution.

Future employment trends now seem likely to lead to a situation of much greater social division unless welfare, education, and work policies are fundamentally changed. Before the turn of the century a much larger proportion of the population—perhaps 30 per cent—will be unemployed, either permanently or chronically; a small elite of professionals, managers, and administrators will hold secure and powerful positions, and the majority of workers will be sandwiched in between, locked into fierce rivalries for jobs, security, and promotion.

In this setting of the communications revolution and growing economic crisis, technical men are in the forefront of change. I defined technical men earlier as those who specialise in solving problems related to complex physical experience in the real world. Historically, the scientist was the prototype of technical man, and he still is. High level computer programmers, systems designers and information scientists are all scientists, trained originally in mathematics and electronics. The cultural prestige now attached to high-level computer work exceeds that given in earlier times to the civil and mechanical engineers or to pure scientists.

In the age of heavy industry, engineers were the most important representatives of technical man; today electronic engineers retain this prestige through their links with computer work. Other technical men are economists, architects and town planners. These vocations are less 'scientific' than other forms of technical work because, for architects and town planners at least, they come into direct contact with people who use their services. The overall attitude technical men have to their work is that of social engineering. Problems are posed and solved in a supposedly neutral, value-free way, just as ABC broadcasts are supposed to be balanced and represent different points of view.

For scientists generally the world is seen as something empirical and measurable. Scientific theories are accepted as valid by international organisations of scientists only when they are based on rigorous methodological and experimental procedures. For computer men, the world is made up of bits of information. Communication engineers successfully measured the information transmission capacity of telephone cables for the first time in the 1940s. The unit of measurement with which they described information was a 'bit'. They were unconcerned with the semantic contents or social uses of information that communications systems might be used for—measuring information communication was merely another technical problem.

The work that technical men are expected to perform is predicated on them distancing themselves from the non-physical dimensions of the work-problems they have to solve. Scientific objectivity develops from a code of professional specialisation which accredits students on the basis of their acquisition of certain codes of proper vocational behaviour. These codes require the systematic reduction of personal bias in solving intellectual problems. Each section of the professional work force—medicine, law, etc.—has its own particular codes for teaching students proper work values and separating them from non-professional workers. The original emphasis on emotional and moral detachment about intellectual problem-solving, however, comes from the work of men in pure science.

It would be difficult to over-estimate the cultural prestige currently given to computers and technical men. People still seem to retain a certain scepticism about scientists and other technical men, but computers themselves are wreathed in a shadowy cloud of glamour and confusion. While humans can only cope with limited quantitative levels of informational complexity—seven 'bits', according to communication psychologist George Miller—computers have enormously high capacities for memorising, retrieving, and processing information.

What computers can't do—and never will be able to—is feel. Low-level computer programmes are often presented to users in what are called 'user friendly' ways. You key the computer in and it responds informally and in a 'friendly' way—'Hi. I'm Charlie, your Orange computer. What's your name?' and so on. Though this personalisation of low-level programmes is only superficial, in some situations people have become psychologically attached to particular programmes.

One U.S. medical experiment linked subjects with a computer that offered psychiatric counselling. Some subjects took the advice seriously, though it had been pre-programmed as projective non-advice, and some were shocked when told they had been dealing with a computer. In other words, people tend to attribute feelings to computers, a cultural process in which media imagery of C-3POs and ETs has been crucial.

Technical men are required to distance themselves psychologically from all information which is not problem relevant. Though there is a tradition of radical, humane scientists who have consistently acknowledged the social responsibilities of scientists—including Australians Sir Marcus Oliphant and Sir Macfarlane Burnet—scientists generally carry over their work attitudes to their politics. They see their role as a-political, neutral or value-free. They also extend detachment as a mode of interpersonal interaction in the workplace. Few technical men's jobs are unionised.

Successful technical thinking requires a sharp division between thinking about something and feeling about it. The codes of scientific objectivity and the moral neutrality of technical work are central credos among the professional elites of industrial societies. Efficiency is equated with intellectual and professional discipline, which is taken as proof of vocational competence and, implicitly, moral worth. Achievement of this level of detachment, however, represses men's capacity for feeling. Gay writer David Fernbach suggests that where women specialised biologically in child-rearing, men specialised in violence, originally through hunting. In industrial society, however, technical men specialise in emotional detachment.

The social engineering to which technical men lend the weight of their professional authority is therefore itself seen as a technical process. With the decline in ideological loyalties in the postwar years, political problems are more frequently seen as technical ones; politicians often justify their decisions in terms of the technical advice of their respective economists, lawyers and engineers. Because technical solutions usually exclude human and political criteria, however, politics organised around technical power does very little about dealing with social inequality.

Official Men: Work as the Rule of Law

In a technologically-based society rationality itself is defined by technical men, but the exercise of social authority is directly regulated by official men. Official men exemplify the publicly-accepted ways of holding and exercising official power. Integrity in role-performance is the public criteria of social competence for official men. A wide range of public images of vocational competence are now described as 'professional'. Actors speak of professionalism no less respectfully than do doctors and lawyers.

Vocational norms traditionally have been described most carefully for professional men. In Australian society doctors until recently stood highest in terms of professional status, while lawyers also hold key roles in the exercise of official power. In most Western societies the relation between law, politics and business has been marked, and no less so in Australia. When it comes to the adjudication of conflict about work matters, lawyers and judges are the final decision makers.

The 'learned professions' originally were considered to be the clergy, medicine and law. With industrialisation a long-term movement towards the professionalisation of official work took place—in conjunction with the expansion of educational and communication systems and the bureaucratic organisation of urban life. Medicine emerged as the most cohesive professional group of the three; the clergy lost its place of prominence; while law as a profession has remained powerful but more internally divided.

Each profession split into 'high' and 'low' levels, with divisions between specialists and GPs in medicine, and between barristers and solicitors in law. Medicine still retains enormous cultural influence in projecting models of legitimate social behaviour. The cultural influence of legalmen, however, is more diffuse but more strategically decisive in regulating social conflict. This is most apparent in the role of the judiciary, a social group to which there is no real medical equivalent.

Where technical men routinely distance their personal motivations in their work, official men mask their behaviour behind professional and vocational roles of integrity. The distinction between masks and persons in the American legal process has been made by one reformist U.S. lawyer, William Noonan. He defines a mask as 'a legal construct suppressing the humanity of the participant' (Noonan, 1976). Social rules create the roles in which authority is exercised, but these roles can and do degenerate into masks. Masks are forms of self-alienation which conceal both one's own self-perception and the perception of others as persons.

Official men routinely engage in masking behaviour. There are political pressures on lawyers which make them specially vulnerable to masking. For lawyers, the judicial system is a branch of the state, and the most profitable and prestigious legal work is to be found in company law. The legal profession is also required to mediate the institutionalised resolution of conflict, but because of its emphasis on tradition and its loyalties to its main employers it is inherently conservative.

Lawyers, especially judges, seek to maintain the idea of the neutrality of the law, just as scientists uphold the objective rationality of their procedures. Studies of the Australian legal profession, however, clearly show there is nothing neutral about the social position of the national legal elite. Judges in the N.S.W. and Victorian Supreme Courts in the late seventies were: all male; previously had almost all practised as barristers; had specialised in commercial and corporate law; 90 per cent had been to private schools; most were members of exclusive all-male private clubs—the Union and Australian clubs in Sydney, the Melbourne or Australian Clubs in Melbourne—and the majority lived in Melbourne's affluent suburbs (Toorak, Kew, etc.) or Sydney's North Shore or affluent eastern suburbs (Vaucluse, Elizabeth Bay, etc.) (Sexton, 1982).

To protect themselves against charges of class bias, lawyers have a formidable set of defences. The law itself is still seen by a majority of the profession as morally neutral. When judges are appointed they are expected to withdraw from public life by resigning from political parties or boards of directors. Ancient rituals also remain important in the self-presentation of Australian barristers and judges, through their wearing of wigs and robes to symbolise legal neutrality.

The process of Australian legal reasoning is itself assumed to guarantee neutrality. English, American and Australian law is much less codified—reduced to core principles—than European law. American law also has broken the traditional British line between barristers and solicitors. The British and Australian system, however, places priority on a tradition of qualitative empiricism in deciding the law. It uses the individual case method via the study of precedent as the substance of its evidence. It also uses the adversary courtroom system of conflict resolution. With this system 'each side prepares its own case independently, then attempts to break down the other side's witnesses by cross-examination, while the judge observes' (Sexton, 13).

Masking becomes operative in legal procedures through the use of language. Lawyers and judges mask their behaviour when they retreat into technical language. The centrality of the interpretation of language is more notable in law than the use of language in any other profession. Every official man's work-role has its own formal and technical language, but debate about meaning and interpretation is a central part of the routine legal process. This is an area where few people in society are qualified (legally) to decide whether such interpretations are justifiable on the basis of law.

Australian lawyers Sexton and Maher quote one 1975 case in this light. In the case of R. *v.* Visiting Justice at HM Prison, Pentridge; Ex parte Walker a long-term prisoner was charged with attempting to escape. The prisoner unsuccessfully requested legal representation in the prison's visiting magistrate's court. He was found guilty on all counts, and later appealed, again unsuccessfully, to the Victorian Supreme Court. His argument was that the magistrate was wrong in denying both the rights of lawyers to practise before a visiting prison magistrate and to deny him legal representation.

The Supreme Court Judge, Mr Justice Hawes, decided against Walker. Sexton and Maher conclude that if statutory provisions of the Victorian Magistrates Court Act (1973) had been given their plain meaning, the appeal should have been upheld. Concerning language, they write: 'It is difficult to avoid the conclusion that the final statutory provision was nullified by means of a semantic device ... there is the vice-like grip of legal logic leading to the drawing of fine but decisive distinctions' (Sexton, 69).

Vocational Identity and Male Authority

Elite and middle-class technical and official men are among the most powerful groups in industrial society. Their vocational process of self-definition gives them great power and expertise in controlling social conflict. Technical men have key roles in legitimating work, while official men have a monopoly of control functions in regulating work. Because middle-class men hold the political power to define the cultural value of work roles and organisational rules, their part in defining male public identity is quite crucial.

Violence is as routinised in middle-class men's working lives as in working-class men's except it is less socially visible. The routine vocational codes of middle-class men encourage distancing and masking as interpersonal strategies for managing conflict. These high levels of self-discipline and self-censorship involve considerable personal costs for elite and middle-class men. Here their own self-alienation is the price they choose to pay in return for reaping otherwise high social and financial rewards. Distancing and masking are interpersonal strategies which exact a price, both from professional men and the subordinate groups they deal with.

So there is a routine level of competitive aggression built into technical and official work which is socially rationalised in a variety of complex ways. Middle-class men use their credentials, language, and expertise in institutional contexts to maintain existing patterns of social inequality. This is not normally their individual perception of their role, but it is the objective social result.

The power of elite and middle-class men, that is, is exercised by influence and discrimination rather than by outright physical violence. Working-class men sometimes have to be openly aggressive to redress their socially subordinate position, but middle-class men express their aggression more by strategic withdrawals from interaction. In industrial relations, when company management want to dominate their workers, they either don't inform them of what's going on, manipulate them behind the scenes, or refuse to meet them.

Where middle-class technical and official men play active public roles in defining models of male vocational and interpersonal competence, working-class men play passive, or reactive roles. But routine media news sources rely heavily on official channels, and working-class men have only limited access to those channels. As I will show in the next chapter, the media reflect and reinforce these dominant personalised images of male identity and cultural authority in class terms. Social distancing is one of the main ways male industrial elites exert power. It is also one of the main functions of the media.

13 Work and the Media

The Australian media report work excellently in some areas and poorly in others. The quality press supplies in-depth coverage of financial news and current politics. Australian financial and political journalists are the elite corps of Australian journalism, and their standards are as high as their international peers. The *Australian Financial Review*, the Fairfax-owned national business daily, is as prestigious in the Australian print media as London's *Financial Times* or the *Wall Street Journal* are in Britain and the U.S.

The commercial media's treatment of other non-business community affairs is made up of its treatment of the public sector—especially health, law and education—and the role of the unions. The same standards of excellence in journalism are not extended to non-commercial community affairs. Rather, public sector activities are consistently downgraded, while through the seventies crude anti-union bias was periodically displayed.

The commercial media divide the world at work into three main sectors—private, public, and the peripheral. Peripheral news is about the media itself, about films, plays, art shows, sport and leisure. This kind of news concentrates on work which is done for entertainment, though the work processes in the media itself are not foregrounded. Sport and entertainment news makes up a major regular part of the commercial popular press and television.

The activities of prominent men dominate financial and political news. Men there are presented as models of success and leadership. Men also predominate, though less completely, in news about community affairs, the public sector and the unions. Men's activities also occupy centre stage in popular sports reporting, while it is only news about entertainment, welfare and leisure which gives women substantial recognition.

Men working in business and politics are framed by the media to model the qualities of successful leadership. In the public sector and in unions, they are expected to behave more as community leaders and as loyal followers. In sports and entertainment they are meant to play a celebratory and symbolically unifying role. The media show men in politics, business and public service as supplying real leadership, while the same moral virtues and values and attitudes are supported in a peripheral context in sports and entertainment. In other words, the cultural function of sports and media men is to act as cheerleaders for the real leaders.

The commercial media's concentration on the affairs of the private sector and their disparagement of the public, work to exclude blue-collar work almost entirely from public attention. White-collar work is presented as prestigious, serious, and worthy of detailed media attention, but blue-collar work isn't. A related difficulty here is the traditional practice of corporate secrecy in withholding information about organisational strategies and procedures to retain a competitive edge.

Businessmen

Despite frequent left-wing criticism that the Australian press is controlled by business interests—which it is—personality profiles of Australian businessmen in the financial press are not always flattering. Especially in the climate of sustained recession, the number of company failures has added an often sombre note to business news reporting. Some businessmen have responded by blaming the media for spreading gloom and doom. Another cultural limitation on presenting businessmen as heroes is that business in Australia is not ranked so highly as in America. Some biographies of Australian business leaders—such as Blainey's life of Essington Lewis of BHP—project a 'captain of industry' image, but others, such as Gavin Souter's history of the Fairfax group, convey a more complex and less uncritically enthusiastic picture.

There is still a series of news stories centred around the activities of leading Australian businessmen. These often strongly make the connection between personal leadership and business success. Many of these are couched in sporting terms and tend to represent the Australian business elite as a British-descended, cultured neo-aristocracy. Their cultural and sporting interests are highlighted by journalists to soften the image of men solely dedicated to making money, as if this is suspect. For example, an *Australian Financial Review* profile of Robert Holmes à Court's part in the takeover bid for

Elder Smith's in 1981 was advertised with a picture of à Court riding a horse. The copy also used sports terms—'key players in the crucial week ... the deceptions, the decisions, the mistakes, and the fumbles'—while the series was billed as: 'THE CORPORATE THRILLER OF THE DECADE' (*SH*, 2 January '83).

Articles about top companies and executives are often written in a factual, straightforward style, with only brief comments on the role of business managers. The *Business Review Weekly*'s story about BHP's controversial purchase of Utah International presents it as a characteristic decision of BHP Chairman, Sir James McNeill, backed up by company lawyer David Adam. Yet mostly it discusses the financial and industrial context of the decision (5 February '83). More colourful businessmen are treated in more colourful terms. Press reports about Alan Bond or Gordon Barton, for example, are more personalised and seek to say something about the character of the men concerned.

Where Bond's political views are to the right, Barton's are to the left. Barton's hard-working, jet-setting lifestyle is foregrounded in media accounts in a predictable way. About the man himself, a *Business Review Weekly*'s profile said: 'Barton is a man who speaks quite openly about anything; business or personal matters, in a quiet, level voice—but still has that ability to convey reserve. He actually shows very little of his inner self' (5 February '83). Barton's cosmopolitan lifestyle is also linked with elite places of residence—Vaucluse in Sydney, Thurlowe Square in London—and some of his previous cultural innovations like the *Nation Review*.

A more maverick figure than Barton, Alan Bond has been beloved by the Australian media for his patriotic involvement in trying to win the America's Cup. A profile in the weekend *Australian* stressed Bond's recent involvement in a plan to sell $1 shares in racehorses to the public. It also reported his emphasis on the need for Australians to work harder, though not necessarily longer; he advocates a 36-hour, flexi-time week, which would employ the capacities of public buildings 24 hours a day. Again an interest in culture is foregrounded—this time by mentioning Bond's friendship with N.S.W. Art Gallery Director Edmund Capon, as well as Bond's own personal collection of nineteenth-century French Impressionists. Asked about the importance of money, Bond responded: 'Money? Money is the measure of the success of your efforts. That's all it is' (29 January '83).

A second level of media talk about businessmen is concerned with the success of new, younger men—either self-made or from business families. A *National Times* profile of Geoffrey Hill, a 36-year-old Sydney millionaire merchant banker, reported his companies' successful merger with one of Britain's largest merchant banks. Like some of the newer sportsmen, a higher-educational background was important to Hill. He studied for a Masters of Business Administration at the University of New South Wales. Hill's company had successfully given corporate advice to the John Spalvins group of Adelaide, as well as to Alan Bond, in engineering some of the biggest company takeover sprees in recent years (19 December '82).

The 'self-made man' theme comes through more strongly in glossy business magazines, such as the *Business Review Weekly*. Their February '83 profile of millionaire Victorian businessman Carl Strachan emphasised the capacity of businessmen to turn the recession to their advantage. 'In the 1930s depression a third of the people suffered, a third rode it out and the other third made a hell of a lot of money,' Strachan said. 'There's heaps of ways to make money ... in a depression you go in even harder' (4 February '83). Again, businessmen are shown as sportsmen and adventurers. Strachan's experience as a Cooktown publican is covered, together with 'his new passion for show jumping' on a ten hectare property at Berwick, Melbourne.

A variation on the new, younger successful businessman formula is the transmission of wealth and financial acumen within Australian business families. The *Financial Review*, for instance, profiled Nigel Corne as representing the third generation in the Sydney Corne family in film exhibition. Corne runs the Hoyts Bondi Plaza Cinema as well as other city real estate properties. His grandfather had been involved in cinema exhibition in the Blue Mountains and previously in England and Wales. Corne's cinema is making a profit because of careful attention to his market and close tie-ins with Hollywood distributors (*FR*, 7 May '82). A similar *Business Review Weekly* story about brothers Marcus and Peter Bourke, grandsons of the legendary land developer T. M. Bourke, explained how Bourke's had successfully invested in the Queensland Sunshine coast property boom, withdrew their funds before the collapse in 1981, and then re-invested in prestigious inner-city real estate in Melbourne (5 February '83).

The third and last level of routine stories about businessmen are about the not-so-successful or those leaving business. These are about businessmen who've either retired, gone bankrupt, aren't doing so well, or have just recovered from insolvency. The *Sun*, for instance, profiled Jack Hannes, founder and ex-Managing Director of Hanimex, leaving the company after its sale to Burns Philp. Hannes had started Hanimex in 1945, but the expansion of the company outgrew his control. By 1980 Hanimex had branches in eleven countries including Ireland, Hong Kong, and the U.S. This international orientation of Australian businessmen is emphasised in media treatments of companies like IPEC and News Corp. (*S*, 4 January '83).

More ambiguous treatment is given to businessmen who have gone into receivership but made a come-back. The *Mirror*'s profile of Sydney commodities dealer Robert Howes touched a mild note of scepticism about his return to business. Howes now holds the Australian agency for Cybercast, an American computerised software package which makes daily recommendations 'to the sophisticated commodities punter'. 'Australia is still great for business if you get your head down and work hard,' Howes was quoted. The *Mirror* concluded its profile by describing Howes as a 'reinvigorated messiah of computerised commodity punting' (27 January '83).

Another step down the ladder of business prestige comes with media accounts of businessmen who've been charged with tax evasion or white collar crimes. The Australian media made very little of these issues until the 1982 Costigan inquiry into 'bottom of the harbour' tax schemes. One group who'd borne the brunt of public inquiry into their company affairs till then had been the Barton family. Alexander and Thomas Barton's company dealings had been under investigation by the N.S.W. Corporate Affairs Commission between 1974 and 1981, at an enormous legal cost, until the charges were finally dropped. A *National Times* account of the background to the Barton case ended up blaming the Corporate Affairs Commission rather than the Bartons. (19 December '82).

Yet there is now considerable uneasiness in the business press about sharp company practices and the proliferation of tax evasion schemes. Despite the abuses of the health scheme by doctors, business frauds are probably still easier to perpetrate in Australia than professional ones. As a *Sun-Herald* profile of international con-man Joe Flynn indicated, Flynn's career as a professional confidence man had involved him in frauds in real estate, oil companies, and selling fake news to major news agencies. According to the story, Flynn had even conned Rupert Murdoch out of $50 000 for a pair of old shoes supposedly once owned by American labour leader Jimmy Hoffa (6 February '83).

Powerful Businessmen and Admen

The power and prestige of big businessmen is partly a result of their association with companies in the most publicly glamorous areas of the economy—mining, oil, energy, the computer industry and communications. Large company chairmen, like Sir James McNeill, have a quasi-ambassadorial role in presenting their companies' activities to the public. *The Bulletin*'s story of the Utah takeover by BHP showed

Sir James negotiating with Australian state premiers, the Prime Minister, senior executives of General Electric—the parent American company of Utah—unions, and rival Japanese coal companies. His accompanying photo shows him as calm and assured (8 February '83). Here BHP and Sir James are intertwined to exemplify the powerful images of Australian business and businessmen.

The prestige of Australian businessmen also comes from their links with major international business elites. The role of big business in postwar resources development has been almost matched by its interest in introducing new computers and communication technology. Australians always have been fascinated with improvements in transport and communication, and in the American-decreed 'information age' the prestige of science and technology belongs to its corporate sponsors. It becomes politicians' jobs to present the new technologies positively to both the business community and the public. On 7 May '82 the *Australian Financial Review* announced 'Sinclair's Open Access Satellite Policy'. At that time the government was guaranteeing open access to the satellite for business and public interest groups, and large-scale manufacturing spin-offs for local industry. Promotion of the new technology to the public requires more of an emphasis on jobs. 'CABLE TV AHEAD WOULD MAKE JOBS', the *Daily Telegraph* reported, repeating claims by Queensland Liberal MP and ex-TV personality, David Jull (29 December '82).

With the new postwar emphasis on communications technology the Australian advertising industry became more strategically important in orchestrating public debate. Australian advertising's main postwar cultural function has been to combine the voices of big business and big government in a mixture of corporate and nationalistic messages. The social norms encouraged by advertising are essentially simple guidelines for efficiency. Corporate advertising projects images of low-profile but immense business strength, the Project Australia campaigns promote working hard and pulling together as simple patriotism, while health and community-oriented ads encourage people to look after themselves and their immediate environment.

The advertising industry is not often reported in the popular media, and only irregularly in the quality press. Like business, it has its own trade press. Where the public image of big corporations and big businessmen is solid, respectable, and usually impersonal, trade reporting of advertising glamorises ad-men. It rarely identifies which agencies are Australian owned, and pushes the theme of advertising men as creative upstarts—or clever larrikins.

This was the theme of a *National Times* profile of Melbourne agency Kurt Skinner Bennett. In 1982 KSB had run a national TV campaign for Brownbuilt office equipment featuring a zany 'Space Invaders' approach. A businessman and his secretary (nothing new there) were shown zapping dirty old shelves into nice new Brownbuilt ones. Agency spokesman Bennett knocked what he saw as the conservative, anti-competitive nature of Australian business. According to him all advertising is unoriginal, but there is great craft involved in re-packing it. This is an excellent definition of most advertising—recycled unoriginality (20 June '82).

The idea of the ad-man as a bit of a lad comes through again in *B&T*'s profile of the then new federal chairman of the Advertising Federation of Australia, Terry Connaghan—'KID FROM THE ROCKS THE TOPS' (1 April '82). In 1982 Connaghan and May's agency ranked number 11 in Australia, after its fortunes had been boosted in 1980 by the sale of 25 per cent of its business to U.S. agency N. W. Ayer. Sales of Australian advertising companies to American firms, like Singleton's lucrative sellout in 1979, are presented routinely as signs of success in the trade press.

Asked about his and the AFA's priorities, Connaghan identified the main one as continuing to 'fight the PKIU battle'. The AFA was opposed to any efforts from the traditional trade union community, in which the printers are an important group, to unionise advertising. The AFA was promoting its own organisation the ACIAA (Australian Commercial and Industrial Artists Assocn.). *B&T* mentioned Connaghan's lapsed Labor Party membership as untypical in the industry—which is solidly pro-Liberal. Connaghan described his own background as 'right-wing Irish Catholic', which makes more sense. Concerning political advertising Connaghan gave qualified approval. 'A political party is a product, and we are professional advocates.'

The growing links between advertising, corporate identity, and politically-funded advertising have received little criticism from within the industry. Chairman of American-owned agency Ogilvy and Mather, Reny Cunnack, said: 'If the Australian government decided we were to have Cruise missiles in every suburb and that decision was enacted in Parliament, I don't see why it shouldn't use an advertising company to explain it' (*NT*, 6 June '82). Some agencies have been less sanguine. Melbourne's Young and Rubicam agency has handled government recruiting campaigns for the armed forces, but disagreed with agencies advertising socially controversial subjects such as the wage-freeze.

Most agencies see it as axiomatic that products will be promoted aggressively. The main exceptions are corporate advertising, community and media promotions, and those particular products where a tough image or campaign wouldn't suit the product. Otherwise agencies speak routinely in the trade press about the need for both aggressive promotion and aggressive marketing by product suppliers.

In the recession in Queensland a number of small local agencies have survived by hitching their star to local companies identified with one colourful sponsor. The relatively low-budget TV commercial, that is, allows the client to play out the hard sell directly rather than the agency having to do it another way. Such simple minded pushiness—'Let Me Do it Right For You', etc.—is the opposite of the corporate image of reserve and impersonality.

Workers

In the seventies the commercial media projected images of corporate power and national unity, and campaigned against inflation and dole-bludgers, yet unemployment was not treated as a major issue. The release of seasonal unemployment figures was reported and given the usual divergent political reception by party spokesmen. At special times, as with the '83 election, the release of higher figures is worth front-page news. 'JOBLESS BURST 10 P.C. BARRIER', reported the *Telegraph* (7 February '83). But normally the commercial media have not focused public attention on unemployment, but have defused the issue.

Reports of ordinary people losing their jobs are not newsworthy unless they can be beaten up as human interest. 'SACK IT TO ME!' was one *Sun* front page (29 November '82). Chilean Maria Hernandez had been retrenched from his job as a process worker. The next day he returned home from the CES to find he'd won $50 000 in the first Instant Lottery Superdraw. This is typical of the flippancy with which the popular media treats unemployment.

Despite the desperate position of many young unemployed people, the popular press uncritically endorses public job creation schemes as adequate solutions, and urges young people on to try harder to get jobs. 'JOBS FOR THE BOYS AND GIRLS', the *Mirror* wrote in its account of the State Government's Youth Corps scheme, and argued 'something was better than nothing'. Part-time work for young people was seen as a means of bolstering self-respect and morale (27 January '83).

On a similarly optimistic note the *Sunday Telegraph* assured its readers 'THERE'S WORK IF YOU REALLY WANT IT'. Four young people were profiled—a window cleaner, a model, a boutique owner, and a freelance advertising copy writer. The emphasis on what is admirable work here falls entirely on white-collar work, with the partial exception of the young window cleaner, who had started his own company. The boutique owner also had got her start through a previous family business in Woollahra. The class-biased mindless optimism of silly stories like this reinforce conventional clichés about how work exists for those who really want it (27 January '83).

Another way the commercial media deflect public attention from unemployment is by glossing over the position of migrants and women in the workforce. The incidence of unemployment is substantially higher among migrants, yet most press treatments of migrant life do not bring this out strongly. An exception is the lot of English migrants who came to work in the steel industry. '20,000 KM TRIP FOR THE SACK', reported the *Sunday Telegraph* of one recent arrival just retrenched at Port Kembla (30 January '83).

Treatment of daily life and culture among the Vietnamese in Bankstown, however, is framed in the *Herald*'s Good Weekend section mainly in terms of cultural assimilation. The article emphasised their desire to be accepted and willingness to work, and briefly mentioned 'racial trouble' in nearby Cabramatta, but said nothing about unemployment. Similarly, the Greek families who own the shops at Sydney's Circular Quay are profiled by the Good Weekend as busy, colourful Sydney identities (24 December '82).

The media's treatment of women in the workforce also has been sharply class-biased and fails to acknowledge the extent of part-time work among women, with its associated problems and greater dangers of retrenchment. Instead, the quality press has presented an image of women determinedly scaling the heights in film, the arts, and the public service. 'PAT LOVELL, GODMOTHER SUPERIOR', in the *National Times* profiled the leading Australian film producer (20 January '82). Although the production side of the Australian film industry is predominently male, the few successful women like Lovell, currently popular actresses, and the rare women directors—Armstrong and Turckiewickz—are held up as models of what's possible for all.

Press reports of the difficulty of ordinary girls getting job are rare. When a 17-year-old girl school leaver had missed out on jobs because of her involvement in the Army reserve, the *Sun* complained 'NO JOBS FOR GIRL SOLDIER'. In contrast, a *National Times* October '82 feature on eight women presented 'BIG SISTER' as competent, successful professionals. This considered the efforts of women in business, education, and the public service to break down male sexism and turn male methods—like the mentor system in job selection—to their own uses. Taken in itself the story is a positive sign of changing times. But set in the context of the media's avoidance of unemployment as an issue, the accumulation of such success stories suggests that women generally are now in a stronger position in the workforce, where the reverse is true (24 October '82).

Public Servants and Unionists

While the media praise the power and wisdom of businessmen and play down the difficulties of ordinary workers, they carry on a fitful sniping campaign against the public sector. The media often associate unions with public sector employment. The at times extraordinary prejudice shown by the media in their treatment of unions is only possible because a consistently sceptical attitude is maintained towards the public sector.

When the Davidson Report into telecommunications came out in October 1982, the quality press widely canvassed the possibility of business taking over the lucrative parts of Telecom services (*SMH*, 29 October '82). But the ground had been prepared well in advance. Back in June the *Daily Telegraph* had been screaming 'TELECOM MEN IN SP RACKET PROBE', about unsubstantiated allegations of links between Telecom and organised crime (12 January '82).

The N.S.W. State Rail Authority also has come under regular fire in the popular Sydney media. 'GOING BROKE!', was the *Mirror*'s introduction to a story about 'that giant multi-million dollar loser', the N.S.W. Railways. Improvements made by the Wran Government to public transport were an important part of its late seventies political image, but the metropolitan press has done its best to undermine it. 'Even hard, experienced Trade Union leaders who went into the service to iron out industrial trouble spots were appalled at what they found,' wrote the *Mirror*'s chief industrial writer, Ray Turner (16 November '82). Later, in reporting the SRA's efforts to solve its problem, the *Sunday Telegraph* highlighted David Hills as saying, 'A victory for the SRA in cutting its costs will be a victory for socialism' (30 January '83).

The public sector in Australia has been used to promote the interests of private enterprise. It has always had a supportive role towards business, not an antagonistic one. Despite this, popular antagonism to the public has been maintained by political conservatives, the media, and a few doctrinaire leftists. Together they sustain a national mythology about public service laziness, waste, inefficiency and privilege. 'HUGE "WASTE" HITS WELFARE', the *Sun* reported in another variant of the theme. According to a management consultant report, N.S.W.

welfare administration was 'top heavy, inefficient, and squanders money' (3 February '83).

There are, of course, elements of waste and privilege in any large bureaucracy, and probably state bureaucracies are more vulnerable to this than private ones. But the wider importance of the negative frame the media uses to identify the private sector is that this is then carried over to its treatment of strikes and unions. Keith Windschuttle has documented monotonously regular cases of the commercial media acting as union bashers in the seventies. Yet his view that the media are always anti-union and anti-strikes is not sustainable. The unions which are most attacked by the media are often those in the public sector. Further, some strikes do not attract media criticism. There are also great power differences between major national unions and the ACTU and smaller unions.

Quality press reporting is aware of these differences even if it does not foreground them. Major unions and the ACTU are recognised as leading industrial organisations and their actions are regularly covered. The quality press accepts unions as qualified players in the industrial relations game, even if they're not the media's favourites. A *Sydney Morning Herald* editorial on unions and penalty rates, for instance, remarked that for the first time in the postwar years the Australian union movement was on the defensive against employers concerning work conditions. That assessment is debateable but the position of big unions is accepted in Australian culture, as is big business. People complain about both, but the government, unions and business are the main actors in most national political scripts.

The quality press is not uniformly hostile to either big unions or to the public sector. It depends on the context. Ian Reinecke's report on the Telecom re-organisation in *Communications*, a Thomson publications new magazine, framed Telecom union activities favourably: 'UNION FIGHT TO RETAIN THE AUSTRALIAN CONNECTION'. To defend themselves against business creaming off Telecom business, ATEA leaders have developed their own public information campaign to show that Telecom is already efficient (September '82). Similarly, the *Herald*'s report on the end of another Sydney train strike was pro-SRA: 'WE "BIT THE BULLET" TO SAVE JOBS' (16 November '82).

Strikes in non-public-sector industries are also not so routinely attacked by the media. The truckies strike of August '82 received fairly sympathetic treatment from the Sydney media, if not from the state police. Apart from John Laws' well-publicised sympathy for the truckies, the truck drivers' campaign to attract public support by staging public blockades around Sydney's main arterial roads was accepted reasonably well by the press. The unnecessary force police used to end the strike, however, took place when media crews were absent (15 August '82).

This is not to say that unions are treated fairly and well by the media. But some are treated more fairly than others. Since the recession has worsened, blatantly anti-union news is no longer so prominent. But the threat of militant unionism is like that of the dole bludger lazing at Surfers Paradise—it is kept on file and repeated on demand. Just as readers of the *Sunday Telegraph* adjust to John Laws' regular union bashing—'INDUSTRIAL RELATIONS: A BLOT ON OUR LIVES' (4 April '82)—readers of the *Sun* regularly see unionists portrayed as aggressive—'WAGE FREEZE: UNIONS FURY' (16 November '82). Anti-union news also persists through sensational reports of overseas union violence, either in America from the Teamsters Union (*S*, 27 January '83), or in *Communications*' profile of Mrs Thatcher's new anti-union hatchet man heading Mercury Communications—the commercial rival of the British equivalent of Telecom—as 'the man who tamed the unions' (September '82).

Education

Education is mainly treated by the media as part of the public sector. Yet of course one of the central political fights about education is the discriminatory funding basis of Liberal governments to private schools. This debate is reported in its own right factually by the quality press, but often framed as a personal conflict between different senior politicians, like knights carrying a favour. 'DAWKINS STAKES FUTURE ON ROLLING PRIVATE SCHOOLS', writes the *National Times* typically (7 November '82). Differences in the standards and facilities between state and non-state schools are not so well reported by the media. When they are, they draw heavily partisan comment from opposing sides.

The commercial press undermines education more by glossing over the differences in the different systems and framing educational news in conventional ways. Educational news in the *Sydney Morning Herald*'s weekly education supplement edited by Spiro Zavros, for example, is politically neutral—like state school education—but it separates school issues off from what is happening in the 'real world'. Meanwhile, reports about education in other sections of the paper are purely factual, but often negative—'N.S.W. SCHOOLS LAG ON JOB ADVICE' (14 August '82). Reporting educational news like this separates it from its context and de-politicises the education issues involved.

The Bulletin regularly carries destructively critical articles about the education system. 'BUREAUCRACY BOGS DOWN OUR HIGHER EDUCATION', writes Tim Duncan. He suggests that higher education administration is out of control, and that universities are on the way to becoming 'badly but not wholly regulated arms of the State'. Duncan concludes by deferentially citing the director of CRA's views on the need for efficiency in management.

Right-wing criticism of education, that is, is commonplace in the quality commercial media. However when books which criticise education from a left-wing perspective are published like Connell's recent *Making the Difference*, the reviews often trivialise them. This particular book rated a six hundred word review in the *Sydney Morning Herald* from Sam Dutton. What Dutton said wasn't specially critical of the book, or very acute. It didn't matter. The review was framed humorously and Dutton was described in the usual reviewer's footnote as 'currently trying to get out of the University of Sydney. He wants to be a gardener when he grows up' (7 August '82).

SMH columnists more openly express their own elitism and indifference to the state system. Yvonne Preston slated education in a Wednesday column 'EDUCATIONS GRAND DREAMS LIE SHATTERED'. She claimed that after Whitlam the high hopes then held for education had declined. This fair comment, however, was made in the context of her assumption of the superiority of private school education. Mistakes in HSC Marking, too much Australian history, and multiple choice exams were mentioned along the way as signs of state education failures. Her throwaway conclusion was: 'It's not the four-term year that teachers want so much as the five-day weekend' (22 June '82).

The commercial media's attempts to pay attention to interpersonal conflict in the schools themselves is secondary to their reports of political conflicts about funding. Otherwise, the popular press takes an inflammatory approach to issues like discipline, bullying and school vandalism. The waves of outer-suburban Sydney school fires owe something to the media publicity they attract, though this is now explicitly referred to and denied in 0/10 *Eyewitness News* reports (12 February '83). Routine media reports about successful sports and entertainment stars often highlight their dislike of school, while media pontificators like Bruce Bond admonish teachers for not being sufficiently realistic (2GB, 8 February '83).

The media's failure to report conflict in the schools seriously is like their failure to report industrial accidents. Industrial accidents and illnesses cause the loss of more working days than strikes, but the media show no interest. The same applies with school conflict. There is a cynicism in commercial media reporting of the educational system which plays on traditional community anti-teacher and anti-intellectual attitudes. At the same time, the media piously complain about a worsening of educational standards and the lack of satisfaction employers have with school leavers or university graduates. The media and educational systems in Australia are not integrated constructively in the way they are in the U.S. They are antagonistic systems, and Australian society and school kids are worse off because of it.

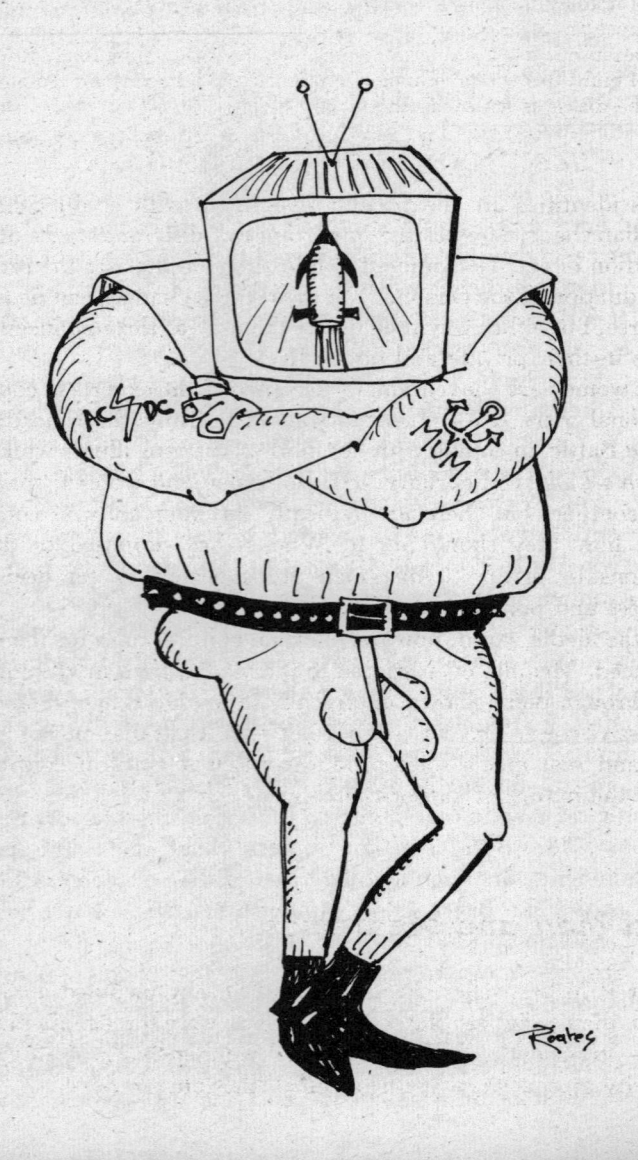

14 Men, Media and Violence

> If mankind commits suicide one day—or day after day—it will do so to music, nuclear war or not... Music is a universal form of communication because it has nothing to communicate... Our most likely future is one of multi-directional non-stop pop music, and the very movement that fills the discos is emptying the lecture halls...
>
> Regis Debray *Teachers, Writers, Celebrities*, 1981

Men's identities are inextricably caught up with conflict and crisis. Freudian theory stresses the importance of different stages of conflict resolution in ego development, while Jung emphasises the progressive individuation of the persona. For men, these changes can be for better or worse, but either way they define themselves through meeting crisis points in their private and public lives.

Yet women are conventionally accepted as the experts in coping with emotional crisis. A *TV Week* story about Lorraine Bayly headlined her 'Brave Battle' in coping with her mother's serious illness while filming *Carson's Law* (12 February '83). Both men and women, that is, deal with conflict, but there are radically different cultural conventions about how they should do it. Women are supposed to deal with emotions in private, while men are expected to act decisively in business and politics in public.

In the media world, however, normal cultural roles for the sexes are displaced. Men are overexposed in the media, both in absolute terms, and through being shown untypically in a wide range of emotionally expressive roles. The discrepancy between Australian media images of men and real men's roles produces a set of cultural contradictions about the nature of authority in society.

Real Men and Mediamen

In her 1976 best-seller, *Passages*, Gail Sheehy included a chapter on men in their twenties. She concluded there were three main personality types—'transient', 'locked-in' and 'wunderkind'. A fourth, but minority group, were men she called 'paranurturers'.

Transient men want to keep their emotional involvements limited. They prolong the experiments of their youth, some constructively and some not. The social group Sheehy identifies as transient are middle-American men of southern and eastern European descent. Transience is unavoidable in migrant life. Locked-in men are more common: these are men who make their commitments in their twenties. They're safe, but stifled.

In contrast, where wunderkind men play to win, locked-in men play not to lose. These kinds of men—sportsmen, young scientists—take risks and often succeed early in their careers. In a competitive culture, Sheehy writes, the wunderkind's most cynical manipulations are willingly overlooked as long as he keeps on winning. They are untiring superachievers. In sharp contrast, paranurturers are men—often bachelors—who spend their time attending to others, such as doctors, teachers and clergymen.

Sheehy's discussion of each type of male identity places value judgements on their behaviour in an individualistic American context. I want to generalise her model to take it outside of that setting, and apply it to Australian life.

In Australian public culture the wunderkind is the dominant male identity. He makes up most of the business and political elite, his job is communication and decision making, and his interpersonal style is one of tough efficiency. Locked-in men, on the other hand, are in business corporations or public sector activities which are administrative or custodial. Locked-in men are concerned with control more than communication, and their interpersonal style is formal.

As paranurturers Australian men play active parts in the public sector or as professionals. They work in health, education and welfare, and their job is to make contact with the public. With the exception of doctors, men working as paranurturers have less social status and cultural capital than either wunderkind or locked-in men, but more than working-class men. The interpersonal style of paranurturing men is unique in male work roles—it is supportive where wunderkind men are tough, and locked-in men are formal.

Last, in a deliberate break with Sheehy's model, working-class men are segregated in middle-class culture as transients. That is, working-class men are seen as unreliable, conflict-prone, withdrawn and inefficient. The culturally dominant models of orderly middle-class identity—tough, formal and supportive—are defined in opposition to the threats of disorderly working-class masculinity. Where the interpersonal role of paranurturing men is soft, working-class men are represented as weak, criminal or brutally violent.

How, then, are mediamen presented in Australian culture,

compared with real men? In the media, soft men come first, especially in the broadcast media. Men like Mike Walsh, Bert Newton and Molly Meldrum are among the most popular mediamen. Tough men—in news, advertising, and adventure shows—come second, while formal men in the ABC (and conventional men in soaps and crime shows) come third. Last, the media shows working-class men either as violent in crime news, or displaces the image of working-class violence to unite the nation against the enemy in foreign war news.

Soft Men: TV Entertainment

Soft men in the media are found mainly in TV entertainment, but also are in children's shows (Simon Townsend, 'Jimmy' in old ABC shows, Jonathan Coleman), writing for women's magazines (Terry Collings), and in some ethnic programmes on 0/28 (Lex Marinos, David Stratton). Sydney radio stations 2CH and 2BL also rely on softly-spoken men, like Len London and Bruce Menzies. Of these, I want to concentrate on men in TV entertainment.

Mike Walsh, Bert Newton, Molly Meldrum and Bill Collins are among the most popular men on Australian TV. What makes them stand out from so many other representations of men in the media is that they are all relatively non-aggressive. Compared with TV tough guys like Tom Selleck (*Magnum*, U.S.) or Dennis Waterman (*Minder*, U.K.), they are soft men. They are also soft compared with the images of Australian TV newsmen like George Negus and Richard Carleton.

Mike Walsh's show also presents other soft men as regulars—Dr James Wright, Richard Neville and John Michael Howson. Wright is the laughing grey-haired doctor who can talk lightly about the worst illnesses. John Michael Howson is the international traveller on a never-ending search for celebrities. Richard Neville, veteran of OZ and IT magazines, keeps casting out his cultural butterfly net.

Walsh's impish style combines humour and intelligence. Ten years on Channel 9 as king of Australian daytime TV has made Walsh's media place unique. His position now is as strong as that of Graham Kennedy in the sixties. Walsh's style of self-presentation is that of Mr Nice Guy, whose genuine pleasantness is tempered with a sharp wit. Walsh is also a skilful manager of his own career with his company, Hayden Productions. 'Despite his image of the genial smiling TV host he is a tough businessman' (*SH*, 6 February '83).

The first Mike Walsh show for 1983 was a composite of material he's used regularly—'You don't touch anything that has been terribly successful for ten years,' he commented. This includes light entertainment, fashion, talks with celebrities, health information, and some discussion of current inter-personal problems.

Because the *Mike Walsh Show* goes live to air, there is a refreshing spontaneity to interpersonal behaviour in the programme, which is something special in Australian daytime TV. When mistakes happen, the audience sees them. Item one, for example, was a *haute couture* fashion show hosted by Sonia McMahon, who seemed nervous. Mike had introduced the parade by emphasising Sonia McMahon's role, but the French show manager present kept dominating the conversation. Mike handled this with tact and finally got Sonia to talk.

Other items featured Noel Paul Stookey, ex-Peter, Paul and Mary singer turned Christian; British theatrical producer Helen Montague, who'd managed Robin Archer's London shows; and Professor Carl Wood talking about genetics and test-tube babies. The most unusual item, however, was a talk with Patricia Stern, a woman who'd advertised herself for marriage. Despite the novelty of the subject, its thoughtful treatment was indicative of the elements of serious social concern in the *Mike Walsh Show*.

Walsh's TV identity remains slightly enigmatic, despite his years on camera. It's hard to know sometimes when he's joking. Perhaps this reflects his own natural reserve. He has succeeded in keeping his private life as a bachelor off the front page. Compared to profiles of Meldrum or Newton, the Mike Walsh personal story is very low-key.

Bert Newton is as lovable as Mike, but more of an out-and-out clown. Newton's position in Australian TV for the last decade could easily have won him solo star billing, but he chose to continue playing second fiddle to Don Lane just as he previously did with Graham Kennedy. It doesn't seem to matter. The *Don Lane Show* is as much, if not more, Bert's than Don's. Newton has a genuineness and an unmalicious sense of humour which makes him one of the great Australian TV comics, surpassed only by Paul Hogan. Newton's relative lack of egoism is rare in a star performer. This may owe something to the difficulties of his early career, which had included a nervous breakdown and alcohol problems (*A*, 12 June '82).

Molly Meldrum and Bill Collins are dominant in presenting rock music and movies nationally. Other rock and picture show hosts come and go, but Molly and Bill seem set to last for ever. Both are experts in their field, and both live immersed off-screen in the culture they present on camera. Meldrum, like Newton, has placed self-imposed limits on his career and ambitions by staying with the ABC. He still manages to drive around in a Rolls-Royce and travels the world constantly in search of Elton John and other stars.

What is so positive about Meldrum and Collins as TV show hosts is their obviously genuine enthusiasm for what they're doing. Molly's mumbling and Bill's gushing get a bit much sometimes, but usually they succeed in bringing a refreshing gentleness to Australian male TV roles (*S*, 13 January '83).

The only criticism worth making of the soft men in Oz entertainment television is that they are an all-male group. Basia Konkowski on 0/28's *Rock Around the World* and Micki de Stoop on 2GB afternoon talk radio are examples of women acting as positive entertainers. But why should mainstream TV entertainment, variety, rock, and especially the atavistic game shows be monopolised by men, when they have large female audiences and regularly use female acts?

Tough men: Newsmen and Politics

Tough men in the media are TV newsmen, political journalists in the quality press, professional sportsmen, rock 'n' roll cockrock stars, the super-smooth DJs of commercial radio, men in war films and in TV police and adventure shows. Tough men are also featured in TV advertising for beer and football, in the Marlboro Man image in outdoor and magazine advertising, and in the ad for Solo as a man's soft drink. Of these, I want to concentrate on political journalism in the quality press and on TV.

Political reporting in the Australian quality press is of a consistently high standard but is often tough, like the men who succeed in politics. As John Tingle said on 2GB in week two of the '83 election campaign—'the nice guys don't survive in politics. You've got to be pretty tough and ruthless' (14 February '83).

Regular political reports are written by Peter Bowers (*SMH*), Mungo MacCallum (*SH*), Neil O'Reilly (*SH*), Phillip McCarthy (*NT*), Peter Robinson (*SH*), Ann Summers (*AFR*), and Marian Wilkinson (*NT*). These journalists provide in-depth analyses of current politics, where writers with literary flair, like Craig McGregor and Peter Corris, are brought in to write more personalised profiles.

Australian political journalism normally offers sensible and well-informed comment, yet it has its own built-in biases. There is an underlying sense of scepticism and acrimony in much political journalism which reinforces the already strong sectarianism of Australian political talk. Second, because of the unique cross-ownership of print and electronic media in Australia, it is extremely rare for print journalists to examine the role of the electronic media in elections, or vice versa. There is an overload of political analysis sometimes, and not enough at others. In contrast, the broadcast media shorten political news and simplify it, while political advertising is designed as a set of cues designed to cut across in-depth analysis and trigger off reactions in already politicised audiences.

The standard charge of politics being reduced to a contest of personalities has been forcibly brought home in the Fraser-Hawke election. Journalists labelled it as the first Australian Presidential election. Peter Robinson spelt his out in the *Sun-Herald* in an article 'THE PHONY ELECTION'. Robinson emphasised the role of TV in political communication, arguing that elections are now being fought on images instead of issues: 'Forgetfulness, engendered by the most overwhelming torrent of words and images in Australian political history, is the way this subliminal effect is being achieved' (13 February '83).

A footnote to this is the election of media personalities directly to parliament. This is a world-wide phenomenon, in India as in the U.S. In Australia in 1975 Brisbane TV personality David Jull became a Federal MP until losing in the '83 contest. More recently, in 1982 Terry Norris, an ex-Sergeant from *Cop Shop* was elected MLA for Noble Park in Melbourne, and the new Labor Premier of W.A., Brian Burke, is an ex-journalist (*ST*, 30 January '83).

A related problem is the emphasis on the military virtues by some political journalists. Another of Peter Robinson's 'Candid Comments' on Hawke's election prospects assessed his leadership potential in military terms. 'He is a leader,' Robinson wrote, 'who is not only the Field-Marshal in supreme command, the political brain and the minister for propaganda, but is also out there in the field storming trenches in person' (*SH*, 13 February '83). Robinson went on to discuss Carter's, Reagan's and Thatcher's leadership policies towards their own military to deduce appropriate clues for Bob Hawke in Australia.

A less noticeable effect of the media on political communication is that TV current affairs shows are now framing everyday life in political terms. That is, as the de-politicisation of the public sphere proceeds, TV current affairs shows are making private experience more public and political. There is a growing level of triviality in TV news shows, as the emphasis on news keeps growing while the number of real stories remain the same. Programmes like *60 Minutes* are the modern equivalents to nineteenth century oddities like *Cole's Funny Picture Book*. The Coles children's annual was a quaint Victorian collection of world curiosities didactically presented as scientific entertainment. Australian TV current affairs shows are becoming like that: they present kaleidoscopic jumbles of odd stories about Australia and the rest of the world as serious news items.

One of the final episodes of the now-finished Channel 10 show *The Reporters*, compered by John Laws, carried no direct political content whatever. It ran together four disparate topics: how an English ex-convict had become a successful playwright; how an Adelaide woman was valiantly pioneering musical vaudeville as community therapy; how Los Angeles babies were subjected to strenuous gym exercises; and how the last of the great Australian touring boxing teams was doing in W.A. (2 November '82).

The theme used to tie these stories together was the 'life is a battle' refrain. In the playwright story, 'Mightier than the Sword', ex-convict Eddie Mowray was presented as a talented reformed tough, saying forcefully that prison life was a jungle. In 'Music on Wheels', the Adelaide lady music therapist was shown as a woman doing her traditional job of helping others. The L.A. 'Junior Gym' piece stressed the bizarre aspects of American child rearing practices. Finally, 'The Last Round' showed professional boxers struggling to make a living to hammer home the 'life is a battle' theme. Fred Brophy, team manager, was shown insisting he'd automatically sack any boxer he couldn't beat.

In *60 Minutes*' first episode for 1983 there was only one political story despite the Federal election. Whether the programme lead-in time was too short to take up election issues, or whether the 'no news' policy is going to be here to stay remains to be seen. There were three stories: 'Fit to Die', about the dangers of getting fit; 'Party Girls' about women's home selling schemes; and 'Power Play', about the Franklin River Dam. These stories were presented by Ray Martin, George Negus, and Ian Leslie, while Jana Wendt was relegated to the show's 'Mail Bag' section.

As with *The Reporters*, news reports in this episode of *60 Minutes* were mainly beat-ups which took unexceptional behaviour and used fast editing, bouncy music, and aggressive interviewing to make the subject matter interesting. In 'Fit to Die' Ray Martin conducted a goulish interview with a woman whose husband had dropped dead from a heart attack during a fun run. Joggers, body builders, and aerobic dancers were all shown as vulnerable. Three intensive care wards at the Bondi Pavilion were shown as a routine but unpublicised part of the City-to-Surf Run.

The threat to ordinary life came out again in George Negus' report on 'Party Girls'. This showed hard-sell American gospel-style promotional schemes being used by Australian women's sales teams. The serious content behind the bizarre surface was suburban isolation and the increasing American cultural pressures on Australians. *60 Minutes* constantly promotes the latter, while excluding it from examination. Although the programme is now sponsored by the Advance Australia movement, the show opened with the tune 'You Are So Beautiful to Me' sung in an American voice—something John Tingle criticised the next morning (2GB, 14 January '83).

Negus' interview with one of the women managers of the sales training teams made little headway into discussing suburban isolation. He asked how it was that, with such promotions, women who were once nervous and withdrawn could become so outgoing and aggressive? (This said with an air of genuine puzzlement and admiration.) Creditably, the lady manager rejected Negus' wording, which he had to re-phrase as 'outgoing and energetic'. The item concluded with Negus talking about how bored housewives were being turned into career girls through a multi-million-dollar industry.

The most divisive and only directly political issue in the show was on the Franklin River. Here *60 Minutes* didn't need to throw dirt to get people angry, as they already are in Tasmania. 'The Greenies' were presented, however, as latter-day descendants of Nimbin, Jim Cairns, and flower-power. One resident of Frome refused to be interviewed, saying 'all you want to do is play on the rift and make it deeper and wider'. To their credit, the *60 Minutes* team left that in (13 February '83).

The new direction in current affairs shows in the '80s may be the transformation of current affairs to highly personalised no-news programmes, along the lines already used by *Eyewitness News*. Hard political comment seems more likely to be left to print journalism and the ABC, while commercial TV treatment of current affairs will make lifestyles a political issue. It may have been co-incidental, but the lead item for *60 Minutes* in 1983 was about physical fitness, while later in the same week Liberal party election advertising featured sports personalities and used the metaphor of winning a race. As Peter Robinson suggested earlier, the new electronic politics are more subliminal than explicit.

Formal Men: Official and Conventional

Formal men in the media are presented factually on ABC TV and radio, and fictionally on commercial TV soaps. Men in ABC programmes like James Dibble act officially, where men in commercial soaps like Shane Porteous (Dr Terence Elliot) act conventionally. Where the ABC creates a factual image of the official Australian community, commercial soaps and crime shows create a fictional, personalised version of the same community. Soft men are supportive and paranurturers, but formal men are locked into official (ABC) and conventional (soaps) role performance.

Auntie's Official Men

Formal men on the ABC project an official image of the world. As the only major publicly-funded media organisation, whose experience goes back to the 1930s, the ABC image has an important ceremonial function for Australians. Men working in traditional ABC programme formats—news, cricket, rural broadcasting, and education—project suitable images of official reliability.

Typical ABC formal men are James Dibble, Geoff Raymond and Huw Evans (news), Allan McGilvray, Norman May and Peter Wherret (sport), and Eric Child, John Cargher and John West (music). The style of the ABC's formal men is sober, informed, and authoritative. On-air ABC organisational members generally play lower profile and more conservative parts than commercial broadcasters. But there is also a greater degree of personal idiosyncracy tolerated among ABC performers. Flamboyance is part of commercial broadcasting, but eccentricity is the ABC's counterpart and its safety valve from the pressures of its usual formality. Sometimes this eccentricity suits the format perfectly—Molly Meldrum, John Cargher—and sometimes it doesn't, as with Clive Robertson's jaundiced egomania.

The ABC's cultural role in Australian broadcasting is mainly preservative. It consciously upholds traditions and ABC performers themselves last longer. I can remember first hearing Eric Child's jazz show almost twenty years ago. There is a greater emphasis on continuity in ABC programming. Commercial programming is as volatile as commercial fashion, but ABC programme co-ordinators have a greater number of long-standing programming responsibilities.

Auntie still occasionally acts as a broadcasting innovator. *Four Corners* came years before *60 Minutes*, and Tanya Halesworth was one of the first women on TV, on Six O'Clock Rock with Johnny O'Keefe. Currently, *Countdown* is still deservedly the top national TV rock show, while Margaret Throsby and Geraldine Doogue compare favorably with Katrina Lee or Kay Stammers. In other words, the ABC is capable of doing some things very well, despite its long-term difficulties since 1975. Yet its performance is frequently well below its potential. To develop this I want to discuss the ABC's coverage of science news.

Robin Williams' *Science Show* on ABC radio has been an outstanding series for the last ten years. The show consistently conveys current science information and issues, set firmly in a social context. It has been a model of excellence in science reporting. ABC TV's treatment of science, however, has been mediocre. Apart from running some important overseas specials, such as Carl Sagan's *Cosmos*, the more usual standard has been set by shows like the 1982 series *Towards 2000*, compered by Sonia Humphries and Iain Finlay.

The dominant attitude *Towards 2000* takes to science is adulatory. It has been naively enthusiastic about any new form of scientific invention, however related to its social context. One edition which featured a respectful report on Aussat—the Australian domestic communications satellite due in 1985—treated the satellite with a simple air of wonder.

This programme began with a scary report on a new U.K. method of administering anaesthetic to children. The opening scenes showed a child struggling in hospital, attempting to avoid an anaesthetist's gas mask. The new technique involved a toy music telephone which concealed the gas mask. Here an initial note of fear was created which was quite unnecessary. The next item then showed Iain Finlay at an ANU physics laboratory. There an Australian research team was working on 'the world's most powerful' high-speed wind-tunnel to test re-entry temperatures for spacecraft. Though it was implied that this research was useful to the American space programme, the main emphasis was on science as dogged, loyal determination. 'The Yanks might have the big money,' Finlay said, 'but they don't have the monopoly on brains.'

The show's third item briefly looked at a new computerised car for disabled people. This was handled to give a sense of light relief, with amusing sequences of car-driver backchat. Science here was associated with mercy. The satellite item followed, giving a much longer report on the technical capacity of Aussat. The justification for the satellite, however, was glossed over by explaining it simply as meeting the needs of outback Australians. No reference was made to the in-fighting which in reality had taken place between commercial broadcasters, the ABC, and Telecom over its potential uses.

The programme concluded on a mixed note of horror and wonder about science. The show had begun with images of a child struggling against a gas mask; it ended with images of a man strapped into a medical face mask. This was a new Swedish method of photographing the brain, which first required the patient to eat a meal of radio-active sugar. Despite current controversies about the appropriate social uses of nuclear medicine, *Towards 2000* treated this subject with more naive wonder (2 February '83). The show also used conventional sexist roles in its choice of presenters. Sonia Humphries covered the most domestically-oriented science reports, dressed in a never-ending variety of fashionable clothes.

Conventional Men in Soaps

Men in soaps are usually younger than in cop shows. Their lives and emotions are predictably tied to their occupation and place in the social hierarchy. The individuality of TV entertainment men fails to carry over to the presentation of conventional men in soaps, who are defined more by the place they occupy in a fictionalised community. Soaps are essentially melodramas which represent idealised little communities intermittently under threat. Where cop shows create a tough, hostile world, soaps show idealised families and communities where sensational threats develop from within.

A Country Practice repeats the old Australian legend about beautiful bucolic country life, where apparent friendliness conceals a Peyton Place type thicket of personal weaknesses and betrayals. The leading men in *A Country Practice* are doctors and a policeman. In *Sons and Daughters* metropolitan life in Melbourne and Sydney is simplified to the fortunes of two families, one big business and one struggling.

What both series share is the routine presentation of the superiority of white middle-class British-Australian cultural values. These are played out in a family, business and professional context supposed to represent the community. Both shows use current social issues as a hook to give them some substance, but this is secondary to the projection of conventional personality models. *A Country Practice* has touched on issues such as Down's syndrome, domestic violence, and homosexuality, while *Sons and Daughters* relies more on its exploration of social difference.

Publicity for both shows boosts the elements of social comments they contain, and some media critics have maintained that soaps perform a positive function in doing this. But cumulatively this takes second place to the projection of squeaky-clean goodness and conventional sentiments. Actors in the show are invariably young British-Australians. *The Sullivans* was a unique high point in Australian TV serial making, but sub-standard shows like *Taurus Rising*, and *Arcade*, as well as the American *Days of Our Lives* and *General Hospital*, are more common.

Taken together, the soaps make up a world of kitsch conventionality where people are presented as cardboard cutouts with electronic halos. The only fictional character of any depth to emerge from the current soap season has been female—Rowena Wallace's 'Super-bitch' Pat Hamilton. The presentation of men in Australian soaps is persistently flat and one-dimensional.

The Cultural Roles of Australian Media Organisations

The claim that the media only reflect reality is often used as a defence by media interests and some media teachers. Media images of Australian men, however, are clearly placed in a different order of popularity than the public organisational images of real men. Soft men are most popular in the media, where supportive men in the public sector and the helping professions are valued less than tough or formal men.

There may be several reasons for this difference. One could be that the media just aren't taken seriously by their audiences. This can be disputed both because people spend substantial amounts of time and money on the media, and because media influence on audiences is indirect and cumulative. Another explanation may be that women audiences are crucial to the popularity of soft men in the media, just as women are essential as clients to men working in real-world nurturant roles. A third could be that many men don't enjoy being tough in the real world, and privately aspire to being more supportive.

Most Australians know the names of Kerry Packer, Rupert Murdoch and James Fairfax. Yet their range of media interests is so vast that it's extraordinarily difficult to analyse the different cultural roles played by the main media groups. A model of how masculinity and violence are communicated through the media, however, at least gives us a new perspective in doing so.

The toughest Australian media organisation, in terms of its public projection of images of masculinity and violence, is Rupert Murdoch's News Corporation. Murdoch himself is the wonder-child of Australian media proprietors. His position here is related to the company's development as the only major Australian multi-national media group. True, Robert Holmes à Court is bidding to get into the same game, but compared with the financial interests of the Packer, Fairfax, and Victorian media groups, News Corporation is at the apex of Australian media business. Unfortunately, Murdoch's organisations all rely on the production of gutter journalism. Scandal, violence and suffering are the news formulas used by News Corporation popular papers, from the *Mirror* in Sydney to the *News of the World* in London and the *New York Post*.

The media organisations which project the most formal images of men are the older, less flamboyant groups, traditionally concerned with quality reporting. Fairfax in N.S.W., the Herald and Weekly Times and David Syme in Victoria, and the ABC are groups of this kind. This section of the media plays a central role in communicating information about politics, business and foreign affairs. Fairfax papers like the *Australian Financial Review*, the *Herald*, Syme's *The Age*, and ABC radio and TV news are the flagships of these organisations. Fairfax broadcasting interests, such as Channel 7 and 2GB in Sydney, also carry over their parent group's emphasis on news and information.

Kerry Packer's Publishing and Broadcasting Group deserves credit for supplying some of the most nurturant images of men through Channel 9 and the *Women's Weekly*. Walsh and Newton are Publishing and Broadcasting employees, as was Bill Collins. Channel 9's continued popularity with Australian audiences is due not only to its being first started and the skill of Publishing and Broadcasting as a media group, but to the softer images of men projected in programming material, from Mike Walsh down to Brian Henderson. Of course the Packer group also produces some very tough images of men, notably in the ruthless promotion of World Series Cricket and through *The Bulletin*. But its contribution to Australian media culture through its foregrounding of more emotionally responsive men, and the moral influence of the *Women's Weekly*—especially during Ita Buttrose's editorship—has been culturally positive.

Yet Australian media culture, as Bob Connell has said, is middle-class culture. None of the media organisations project working-class or minority culture positively. Instead there is a range of specialist services. 2KY and 2WS play to Labor and western suburbs audiences, while the trade union movement has its own internal media. Channel 0/28, Radio 2EA and the foreign language press cater for Sydney's ethnic audiences. Adult educational broadcasting in the city is handled by 2SER-FM, and parts of JJJ programming. JJJ-FM also reaches large numbers of younger western suburbs listeners, as the station's signal is strongest in that area. Last, there are the public music broadcasting and religious FM stations, 2MBS-FM and 2CBA-FM. The non-middle-class media, like working-class and ethnic culture, are relatively isolated from the mainstream.

Any model simplifies reality, and significant exceptions to the general pattern of influence outlined here can be found readily enough. However each organisation has a secondary emphasis as well. News Corporation publishes quality papers too, like the London *Times* and *The Australian*, and prestigious lifestyle magazines like the *Village Voice* and *New York Magazine*. Similarly, Fairfax publishes the *Sun*, which often is as sensational as any of the Murdoch papers. Despite these qualifications, important differences do exist in the way the Australian media communicate cultural standards about masculinity and violence.

Media Men and Real Violence

The meanings the media attribute to violence are ordered around a set of overlapping media frames. These frames, or ways of ordering symbolic experience, are dynamic and change over time. They also vary at any time in and between media. Yet the current practices of the media in communicating cultural information still can be explained in terms of their systematic presentation of a series of selected images about men and violence.

The media's projection of images of soft, tough and formal men in entertainment, politics, community life and soaps, is diverse but positive. When media frames are shifted to consider crime and war news, however, men there are treated as the enemy. By doing this the media selectively highlight violence along class and cultural lines to maintain the legitimacy of middle-class and state authority. It also discredits working-class challenges to authority.

These challenges are treated straightforwardly enough in media coverage of work and industrial news. But when it comes to the treatment of crime and war, fears about working-class violence are symbolically condensed and displaced. The image of working-class life is first de-contextualised, and then reconstructed as a framing metaphor for crime and war news.

Instead of the threat to society being identified as working-class violence—viz., strikes and industrial unrest—it is seen as the indirectly related threat to the community of crime. At the next level of displacement, the threat to the nation is war. Considered this way, violence is a story constantly retold by the state through the media to justify its existence, regardless of the politics of the day.

Journalists also have to use a narrower range of sources in writing about crime and war. In routine power struggles within Australia, at any time a variety of competing pressure groups are ready to act as media news sources. But in crime news these official sources are confined to the prison department and the warders' union; the only non-state sources are prison activists and a few groups representing prisoners, like the Prisoners' Action Group. This drastic imbalance in competing sources of information heavily slants crime and war news in favour of the state's official policies.

Crime News: Katingal or Cop Shop?

Images of crime and community life are culturally inseparable in the Australian commercial media. Real crime is constantly shown as a threat to the community, while fictional crime stories show the social context of crime as little communities under siege or at risk. Real crime reporting in the Sydney popular press and on TV has oscillated between neglect and overkill through the seventies.

Dave Brown's study of crime news reporting shows that at the peak period of unrest in state prisons, from 1975 to 1979, the press fabricated accounts and rewrote the public record about events at Katingal and Maitland gaols. Media sensationalism in turn was used by prison officials to deflect criticism at the time of the Nagle Commission Report. Other abuses in crime reporting have been the judicial invocation of an archaic law to protect the *Mirror* from being sued for defamation by prisoner Darcy Dugan in 1979. The same year, the Australian Press Council took no action over false information in a *Sydney Morning Herald* article which repeated the views of prison officials about the banning of *Contact*, a prisoners' magazine.

Generally, quality press reporting about crime follows the story of prison politics, and currently the N.S.W. Ombudsman's criticism of police procedures, fairly reliably. Popular press reports on crime, however, consistently frame complex issues in simplistic sensational terms—'BEER ON THE RUN FOR ESCAPED PRISONERS' (*Brisbane Sun*, 1 February '83); 'CRIMS GO FREE AS POLICE CLOCK OFF' (*S*, 4 January '83); 'ATTEMPT TO RUN DOWN DETECTIVES'. They present any form of violent crime as evidence of an imminent criminal Armageddon—'VAN GANG RAM BANK' (*S*, 4 January '83); 'ATTEMPT TO RUN OVER DETECTIVES' (*M*, 30 December '82); 'CAR BOMB RIDDLE' (*S*, 4 January '83).

A special place in sensational crime news is given to terrorism. The Hilton bombing, the assassination of a Turkish consul-general, and the 1982 bombings of the Israeli Consul and the Hakoa Club in Sydney have been the only Australian postwar events of terrorism. These incidents however led the state and federal governments to form the Tactical Response Group in Sydney and the Special Operations Group in Melbourne as counter-terrorist groups. The TRG has since been used in Sydney to raid a hotel for drugs and gambling. Recent attempts to hijack a TAA jet provoked Murdoch's new Brisbane daily, *The Daily Sun*, to feature the bomb threat—'SAS IN FRONT LINE TO COMBAT TERROR—CABINET FEARS MORE THREATS ARE INEVITABLE' (3 February '83).

While crime reporting in the print media has been politically biased and sensationalist, the fictional representation of prison and police life on TV has been routinised and sentimentalised.

The Australian police historically have had a moral role to play in Australian community life which has been larger, and more open to exertions of moral influence, than that of the U.S. or U.K. police forces. The favourable presentation of this big brotherly type of moral role for Australian policemen has been repeated ad nauseaum in Oz TV crime shows from *Homicide*, through to *Copshop*, *Matlock Police*, *Division Four*, and currently in *Waterloo Station*. As Fiona Manning said in the Sydney *Sun*, the last thing this country needed was another cop show.

In these police shows policemen are humanised, and shown as sometimes heroic figures, while criminals and prisoners are shown as viciously desperate, sadistically cruel, or as figures of fun. No convincing police character stands out in this enormous amount of fictional police footage, except perhaps for *Copshop*'s Glen Taylor and Ray Barrett's brilliant film portrayals of sadistic racist policemen (*S*, 8 December '82). The most memorable characters in the cop shows have been some of the women in *Prisoner*.

War News: I Read the News Today, Oh Boy

The presentation of war news in the media is surprisingly widespread. Foreign news is often framed as military conflict, while entertainment media use war as a staple subject—from *Star Wars* to *The Sullivans*. The commercial media are more likely to promote aggressive nationalism and militarism in their war news treatment, but the ABC does its share in its own quiet way. The ABC relives the military exploits of the past, and repeats orthodox state views of present conflicts. Auntie's militarism is patriotically low-key and very British stiff-upper-lip; the commercials are more Americanised, sensationalised, and as likely to show George C. Scott as a power-mad General Patton as a victorious General Montgomery.

The evening press routinely uses historical features about past wars—'TURKS SLAUGHTERED BY FLYING CORPS' (*S*, 27 January '83); 'SUB-BUILDERS GIVE NEW DIMENSION TO MODERN WARFARE' (*M*, 3 February '83). Advertising also promotes war material. Time-Life Books heavily advertised a new series of books about men at war by featuring a young Kamikaze pilot on his way to battle. TV and the press also routinely carry army advertising—'MAKE A CHANGE, Join the Army Reserve' (*T*, 6 December '82).

The Falkland Islands war of mid '82 involved Australians through their traditional links with Britain. This was very much a radio war for the media, as the isolation of the Falklands was too great for most TV crews and print journalists. Sydney radio at the time was full of war news, especially 2GB. At one point ethnic radio 2EA was directed by the Special Broadcasting Service to stop broadcasting live interviews with people in Argentina (*SMH*, 21 May '82). But mostly the Australian media showed the war as a patriotically loyal enterprise, as the Tory Government did in Britain. There the excesses of the Murdoch British press were eventually censured by editors of other London papers.

The war regularly rated front-page treatment in the press. 'SUICIDE JETS HIT WARSHIP', reported the *Sun* on 26 May 1982, set alongside the paper's announcement of a new game of Super Bingo. Anti-Argentinian comment became standard in both press reports and journalistic comment. Columnist Cirrel Greet wrote in the *Sun*: 'a report says Argentinians think that the Brits are "as mean as Nazi war criminals". Guess the Argentinians should know...' (26 May '82).

Quality press attention to war news, however, is more normally concerned with American–Russian confrontations. A recurrent theme touching on science fiction is the threat of satellites being used for a space war—'WAR IN SPACE: A REAL SCENARIO' (*SMH*, 22 November '82). World news in the *Herald* sometimes is made up entirely of nuclear war news. In December '82 the paper printed 'a key to deciphering the puzzle of News Nuke-speak', which explained military terms like MAD, MARV, MIRV, and X-Ray Blow-offs (28 December '82). Soviet involvement in the now three-year-old invasion of Afghanistan is also remembered periodically—'THE WAR THE SOVIET UNION CAN'T WIN' (*SMH*, 28 December '82). Most of these reports are taken directly from the *New York Times*.

So far the Australian press has minimised the resurgence of the anti-nuclear arms movement in Western Europe, and in England where church leaders have become bitterly divided on the issue. The particular importance of the West German experience has mostly been overlooked by the Australian media, though West German opposition to American plans to deploy medium-range nuclear missiles in Europe has been intensive. A *Newsweek* poll in January '83 found that 57 per cent of West Germans favoured a neutral Europe (*NT*, 13 February '83).

Despite the madness of nuclear war, the Sydney quality press still runs war news features in a sentimentally chauvinistic way. The *Herald*s Good Weekend section uses war as a source of human interest material. 'LAST LETTERS FROM THE FALKLANDS', was the title of a story based on a series of love letters from a young British naval lieutenant killed in action. Accompanying were pictures showing a sinking ship and the sailor's wedding (30 October '82).

A month later the Good Weekend profiled three Australian Chiefs-of-Staff as 'BENNET, LEACH, AND EVANS WAIT FOR AN INTERESTING WAR'. Paul Byrnes' profile of Air Marshall David Evans, Lieutenant-General Phillip Bennett and Vice-Admiral David Leach was a lifestyle treatment, personalising the armed forces leaders. Evans and Leach, however, defended the Australian involvement in Vietnam. Leach was described admiringly as: Vice Admiral David Leach, AO, CBE, MVO, RAN, 'looks like governor material in his white suit and matching hair. His manner is gubernatorial and he is the only one of the three who likes the social whirl' (4 December '82).

Another variant of pro-war news is the intermittent running of spy stories or exposés of political journalists with foreign involvements. The radical section of the quality press is more likely to present the former, while *The Bulletin*'s scathing profile of Australian foreign journalist Wilfred Burchett is an example of the latter—this was syndicated from *Commentary*, a conservative New York magazine (*B*, 17 November '81). In contrast, Evan Whitton, ex-editor of the *National Times*, recently wrote a *Herald* series on 'the world of spooks', which concluded that Australian intelligence organisations had suffered under the Whitlam government, but had boomed since then (*SMH*, 28 January '83).

Australian film culture also has made some input towards a pro-militaristic climate. Neither *The Odd Angry Shot* (Vietnam) nor *Gallipoli* (World War I) made much of the intense opposition to those wars in Australia at the time. The Murdoch–Stigwood film *Gallipoli*, in particular, directed by Peter Weir and written by David Williamson, was a celebration of the masculine virtues of young men joyously going off to war. Anti-war comments in films like these, as in *Breaker Morant*, were so subtle as to be imperceptible. None of the major commercial films about Australians at war, nor TV series, has looked at war as critically as David Bradbury's 1979 film *Frontline*, which was finally screened by the ABC in early '83.

More typically, ABC TV has a high output of British and Australian war programmes. Documentaries like *The Fall of Singapore*, *Task Force South* and a forthcoming study of Australians on the Burma Railway, present official ABC and BBC perspectives on war as contemporary history. ABC news magazines also routinely cover army news—a TV item on Army cooks talked brightly about 'young soldiers sustaining with style' (13 February '83). Senior management and performers in the ABC are more likely to be older men than those in commercial TV, and have had wartime experiences. When Buzz Kennedy's first edition of the new ABC news programme *Midday* went to air, he highlighted an interview with Nancy Wake about the recent arrest of a Nazi war criminal.

The ABC's authoritative role in presenting war programmes needs to be seen in the context of its ceremonial role in Australian culture. Because of its direct links with the state, the ABC's past is professionally inter-connected with British culture, British royalty, and the BBC. This is witnessed by the large amount of BBC programming used, and the higher proportion of English employees in the ABC compared with the commercials. National political announcements, coverage of Royal visits, parliamentary broadcasting, and coverage of major national sports events—like the Brisbane Commonwealth Games—are tasks routinely expected of the ABC.

In this setting, the ABC's presentation of other wartime entertainment programmes, like *Dad's Army*, *We'll Meet Again*, and *Airlift*, is part of its long-standing support for British culture. British comedy, of the BBC 1 variety especially, remains popular on the ABC. Shows like *The Two Ronnies* and *Till Death Do Us Part* get their laughs out of close-to-the-bone sexist and racist humour. Gay pressure groups have complained to the Anti-Discrimination Board in N.S.W. about shows like *Upstairs*, *Downstairs* for using anti-homosexual material for laughs, while the Australian Consumers Association singled out *Benny Hill*'s treatment of women for special criticism. Sexual material in these shows is not directly connected with war, but it panders to sexual intolerance in its audiences, and reinforces chauvinistic and anti-homosexual attitudes.

Conclusions: Male Identity and the Media

The dominant organisations in industrial society supply the dominant personality types. They project the public image of four main groups—the business and political elite, the private and passive public sectors, the active public sector, and the working class. The male identities, or personality types, of men most valued by these organisations, in descending order of prestige, are tough, formal, supportive and weak. Media organisations, however, project a different scale of cultural values, with soft men as most popular, followed by tough and formal men—who are still approved of—and working-class men (or hostile foreign powers) who are ambivalently shown as criminally weak or dangerously violent.

As interpersonal models, the Australian media dislocate the range of roles real men can choose from. It's OK for men to be soft in TV entertainment, the media says; it's also OK for men to be tough in politics and business, formal in their community roles, and conventional in their social and family lives. On the other hand, in the real world it's not OK for men to be soft—unless they're doctors—to be homosexual, not to work, to go on strike or to commit crime.

The symbolic exclusion of working-class men in Australian media culture is taken for granted, as is the selective highlighting of class violence in the framing of industrial and crime news. The media's symbolic condensation of the world uses internal cultural divisions between middle- and working-class men as its organising principle, and then reproduces these, at a different level, in its construction of war news. Militant patriotism is intended as ideology to unite Australians against foreign aggressors, just as aggressively anti-gay humour is supposed to unite real men against homosexuals.

Where working-class men's culture is shown as brutal, weak, or violent, middle-class men's culture expresses aggression in formal or tough male behaviour. Because middle-class values are publicly dominant, however, this kind of aggression is not recognised as a problem. Instead it is institutionalised in organisational communication, and in the ruling elite's cultural control of public debate. Middle-class men have a variety of manipulative interpersonal strategies to protect their power, such as withdrawal, distancing and masking.

Middle-class male cultural dominance leads to the repression of other groups. In interpersonal relations, gay men are rejected, women are dominated, and working-class people are exploited. Politically, the gay movement is co-opted, women are selectively incorporated into public life, and working-class culture is both nationalised and isolated by the state and the media's joint control of sport and gambling. As the Reverend Vernon Turner once said, 'these are serious times. We'll talk about that after this break' (CBA-FM, 21 March '83).

Admittedly, to summarise the media's cultural functions as neatly as this simplifies reality. In a psychological, instead of political sense, the media are very much a mirror reflecting the projection of all major cultural issues. They constitute a complex, shifting, and often surreal landscape of the inner concerns of the present. Considering that men play such important parts in the media as producers, actors and audiences, however, it seems odd that until now the subject of masculinity itself rarely has been discussed in media criticism.

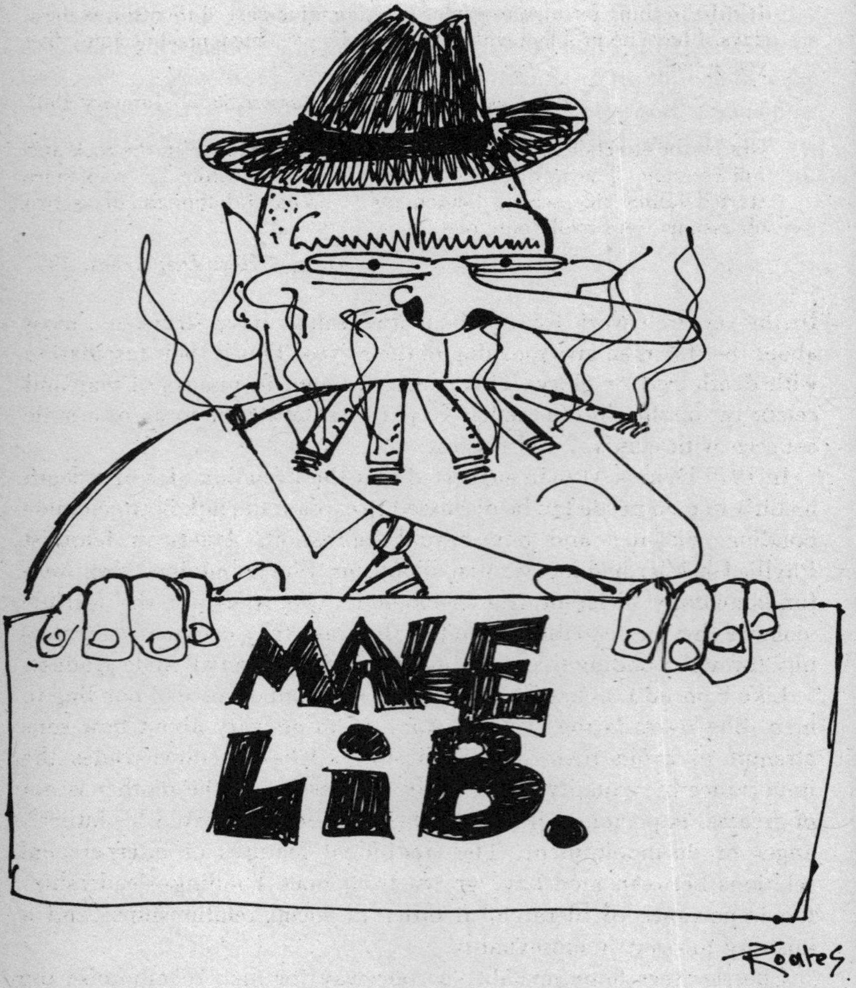
MALE
LiB.

15 Alternatives

> It's the in thing for men to explore the feminine part of themselves these days. I have no problem with that. My wife gave me a machoectomy five years ago.
>
> Bill Cosby *The Johnny Carson Show*, January 1983

> Out on the streets I couldn't tell the Vietnam veterans from the rock and roll veterans. The war primed you for lame years while ... rock stars started falling like second lieutenants... What I'd thought of as two obsessions were really only one.
>
> Michael Herr *Dispatches*, 1977

In the research work for this book two things have struck me most about the way men give meaning to their lives. This is their fascination with death and/or glory. This comes through in images of war and celebrity-worship in the media. In personal terms it's more of a male concern with survival and success.

In 1979 Dennis Altman suggested that the Freudian idea of a death instinct in men needed to be discussed to explain the link between male bonding, violence and homosexual repression. American feminist Phyllis Chessler had just written about this. She maintained men were fundamentally different from women in two ways—in the terrible violence they are capable of, and in the ways they can achieve fraternity through bonding (i.e. working and socialising in all male groups).

Like Konrad Lorenz, Chessler stresses the importance of bonding to men. She re-reads the Oedipus story as an allegory about how sons attempt to avoid their father's hostility. Chessler downgrades the importance of sexuality in the myth. Possession of the mother is not of greatest importance: it is more the son's desire to avoid his father's anger or disappointment. The traditional features of interpersonal relations between men have grown from male bonding—leadership, the importance of hierarchical order in social relationships, and a hostility to overt homosexuality.

Chessler sees homosexuality as one way for men to minimise the potential violence inherent in organised masculinity. So hostility to homosexuals, in turn, becomes a central part of identity formation for the majority of men. It is easier to say what a man is not than what he is or should be. This renunciation of overt homosexuality by men is sublimated into a devout obedience to rulers—the men who are kings, presidents and prime ministers. Men fall into unequal power relationships because they feel a need to relate to each other with either undue defensiveness or exaggerated dominance.

Men's concerns about death and conflict with other men are also part of the establishment of their own identities. The commonsense attitude that men should be tough has this much truth in it—men, and women, develop their personal identities by dealing with crisis situations. Whether the period of conflict occurs most in adolescence, mid-life or senescence, men experience periods of intense personal introspection when they have to check their own self-image against their real place in the world.

But men's age-old habit of seeking out conflict as a means of self-identification has become unprecedently dangerous in a nuclear world. This century already has seen some of the world's largest and most horrible wars. Yet the horrific loss of human life in the World Wars, Korea, Vietnam, the Middle East, Nigeria and Indonesia is overshadowed by the contemporary threat of nuclear war.

After the 1939–45 war American author Glenn Gray examined how GIs dealt with their postwar sense of guilt about killing other men. He concluded that soldiers in war fell in love with their machines and became like them. In one case, a hardened German tank captain broke down and cried after the loss of his tank. Men in combat, Grey argued, become like their machines—automatons devoid of a sense of moral responsibility.

This doesn't happen overnight. It takes a series of repeated brutalising experiences, like boot-camp training, the shock of first combat, the loss of one's comrades, and the grind of combat fatigue, before men become thoroughly de-personalised in war. Even then, as the concentration camp experience shows, humanity and the will to survive still hold some men and women together while others die.

On a different, but psychologically related cultural level, men's preoccupation with success is as strong as their fascination with violent conflict. In the media this is expressed as an endless interest in international celebrities. Bing Crosby, Grace Kelly and Elvis Presley all have had their pasts minutely dug up by the media. Now it is a growing media practice to make programmes about ageing celebrities still alive in anticipation of their death—as a recent *60 Minutes* profile of Laurence Olivier did.

Yet the effects of celebrity worship on modern culture are something that remain largely unexamined. David Thomson, an English film critic, has argued that mass audiences hate their stars as well as love them. More accurately, where political leaders are feared and respected as celebrities, entertainment stars are loved and resented.

When Peter Finch—whose last role was as TV executive Howard Beale in *Network*—died before the film's release and Oscar night in March 1977, Thomson argues there was little doubt he would be awarded the Oscar. This was death enshrined as the proper destiny of stars.

Men's fascination with celebrity as well as war, then, may be based on a common underlying concern men have about death. Death, at least in idealised and dramatised form, has a perennial cultural appeal for men, just as birth has for women. Yet in eyeryday life men usually aren't at war or on TV. Instead they're working—if they have jobs— and the dominant model of work is the organisation. Modern business and state organisations are run as tough, efficient and formal—or as if they are. The problem is how men can overcome the malaise of a society organised around impersonal, bureaucratic institutions. Soldiers become de-personalised in war, while in industrial work conditions they become alienated.

Ancient Chinese society had its own vast bureaucracy, but men also had the teachings of the sages against which to measure their personal experience. Chuang Tzu said that all men were liable to eight defects:

> To take the management of affairs that do not concern him is called monopolising. To bring forward a subject that no one regards is called loquacity. To lead men on to speeches made to please them is called sycophancy. To praise men without regard to right or wrong is called flattery. To be fond of speaking of men's wickedness is called calumny. To part friends and separate relatives is called mischievousness. To praise a man deceitfully, or in the same way fix on him the character of being bad, is called depravity.

Today western men have no such clear guidelines to follow, unless they belong to an organised religion. In industrial culture the media take the part of the sages, except that meaning is constructed in the media by thousands of producers and mass audiences. Though modern culture does not have the authority of the Chinese sages, neither is it any longer patriarchal. We still have a male-dominated, violence-prone society, but Western women—even in Australia—have much greater independence than before.

Before the Australian bush legend declined it peaked in the 1890s, with the *Bulletin*, Henry Lawson, the bushman, and the birth of the 'Man From Snowy River' legend. Hopefully the greater cultural visibility of aggressive men in the last ten years is a sign of the same thing. Perhaps all the images of ugly Australian men—the ocker, the macho, the S/M clones, the Marlboro Men—are being worked through. The ugliness of some of these images, however, is as much a part of middle-class men's cultural projections. Middle-class men remain as locked into cultural models of aggressive behaviour as ockers.

There still are signs of a gradual softening of Australian male public images. Australian films have begun to produce a few images of men that are soft, such as *Lonely Hearts* and *Monkey Grip*. American male stars like Dustin Hoffman, Al Pacino and Jeff Bridges also now appear on Australian movie screens playing homosexuals, transvestites, ex-war vets, and divorced fathers. The adventurer (Harrison Ford) is still there, and so is the tough guy (Sylvester Stallone), but new softer men are visible too.

There is also greater emphasis on the value of communication in Australian society. Some of this is self-seeking, but the 1983 election has seen Bob Hawke stressing the importance of consensus and communication in Australian public life. He has been one of the few Australian politicians to have acknowledged his emotions in public. He even has cried publicly. At his best, Hawke shows that genuine communication must be emotional as well as intellectual.

Another positive indication is the renewal of the conservation movement, with the Franklin River dam issues becoming a national cause. Some conservation groups have also extended their commitments to include opposition to nuclear war. There is also more social awareness of the importance of relating technological change to human needs, as in the popularity of Barry Jones' book *Sleepers Wake*. There are also the slow movements in schools to introduce mass media and interpersonal communication courses.

Another avenue to be explored is media reform. Australian public campaigns so far have centred around children's TV, Labor challenges to monopoly ownership, public broadcasting, and BUGA-UP's war against the outdoor advertising of liquor and tobacco. In fact, advertising needs to be recognised as being as much in need of public regulation as the media. Just as the media project anti-social models of interpersonal behaviour, advertising sells real and potentially anti-social products.

There should be a complete ban on the advertising of alcohol and tobacco, while the backyard cultivation of marihuana should be legalised. In the interim, alcohol and tobacco companies should be taxed to finance public health care directly. Similarly, so long as commercial television allows children's programming to be dominated by anti-social advertising, they should be taxed to fund public child-care facilities.

A more positive change would be the dedication of any new second ABC national TV channel to genuinely public use. It should be technically co-ordinated by the ABC, but involve equally business, education, the unions, and public broadcasting groups. Australian media culture needs constructive changes to bring it together, not to further consolidate existing interests. Channel 0/28 also should include regular Aboriginal programme content, cover British and American culture to bring out its differences from Australian, and show more of non-middle-class migrant life. Last, political advertising should be banned from the broadcast media, and the ABC should be included under the provisions of the Freedom of Information Act.

It is much harder to suggest how Australian men might change to become more open about themselves. Australians badly need to find new ways of talking about themselves and the world, which are not British or American. There is a great Australian folk tradition of storytelling, which needs to be adapted to more personal means of self-expression. People's emotional range is reflected in the language they use.

Perhaps men's involvement in child-care is the most important long-run issue. The best way for men to recover their repressed emotional selves is simply by becoming willing to be involved in the upbringing of their own young children. Changes in the economy now are quickly changing traditional working roles and routines. Men's working lives need drastic re-adjustment so they can spend substantial amounts of time caring for their own children. Men should have the same rights to paternity leave as women, at a slightly later time. If men are ever going to learn how to deal with their violence constructively, then probably their children can best show them how.

In the meantime, we have to live in a world in which new forms of gratuitous and diffused violence—what Italian theorist Franco Ferrarotti calls 'slow violence'—keep cropping up. Modern violence is cultural as well as political, economic and personal. When Bruce Feirstein, the American ex-advertising man who wrote *Real Men Don't Eat Quiche*, and his Australian mouthpiece Alex Buzo joke that 'the movie of the week on the ABC is about a blind 18-year-old rape victim who can't decide whether to have an abortion or join the women's professional golf tour' (*Australian Playboy*, June '82) we have to say no—Not Funny. If some men still think rape is something to joke about, then those of us who don't think so will have to keep saying no, even at the risk of not being seen as really real men.

Anyway, as Joe Jackson says, now and then you wonder who the real men are...

References

This reading list is ruthlessly selective. There is so much available on the media—especially American media—but many sources are of only limited academic value. For purposes of brevity I have included only those items which are directly relevant to the arguments of this book. More comprehensive media references are available in recent Australian texts, such as Mayer (1980) and Bonney and Wilson (1983).

Chapter 1

Allen, Y., 'Women's Hostility', in F. Moorhouse (ed.), *Days of Wine and Rage*, Melbourne 1980.
Altman, D., *Coming Out in the Seventies*, Sydney 1979.
Connell, R., *Ruling Class, Ruling Culture*, New York 1977.
Debray, R., *Teachers, Writers, Celebrities*, London 1981.
Dixson, M., *The Real Matilda*, Melbourne 1975.
Ferrarotti, F., 'On Violence', *Social Research*, 48, 1981.
Goffman, E., *Interaction Ritual*, New York 1967.
Klapp, O., *Currents of Unrest*, New York 1972.
Lefebvre, H., *Everyday Life in the Modern World*, London 1972.
Lewis, G., 'Violence and Australian Nationalism', *Arena*, 43, 1976.
Marcuse, H., 'Aggressiveness in Advanced Industrial Society', in *Negations*, Boston 1969.

Chapter 2

Beilby, P., *Australian Music Directory*, Melbourne 1981.
Frith, S. & McRobbie, A., 'Rock and Sexuality', *Screen Education*, 29, 1978.
Gerbner, G., 'Education About Education by the Mass Media', *Educational Forum*, November 1966.

Chapter 3

Dunstan, K., *Knockers*, Melbourne 1972.
Higgins, C. & Moss, P., *Sounds Real*, Brisbane 1982.
Johnson, L., 'Radio and Everyday Life', *Media, Culture, and Society*, 3, 1981.
Lewis, G., 'Ockerism and Conservatism', *Overland*, 78, 1979.
Lull, J., 'Radio Listeners' Electronic Media Habits', *Journal of Broadcasting*, Winter 1981.
Olson, W., *Baume: Man and Beast*, Sydney 1967.
Rumble, R., *Radio Replies*, Sydney 1936.
Schwarz, T., *The Responsive Chord*, New York 1973.
Spearrit, P. & Walker, D., *Australian Popular Culture*, Sydney 1979.
Webb, E., *Do You Remember?*, Sydney 1942.

Chapter 4

Atyeo, D., *Blood and Guts*, Sydney 1979.
Caldwell, G., *Entertainment and Society*, Canberra 1977.
Cashman, R., *Sport: Money, Morality, and the Media*, Sydney 1980.

Hall, S., 'The Treatment of Football Hooliganism in the Press', in Ingham, R. (ed.), *Football Hooliganism*, London 1978.
Harris, S., *Political Football*, Melbourne 1972.
Hoch, P., *Rip Off the Big Game*, New York 1972.
Nowell-Smith, G., 'TV—Football—The World', in Bennett, T. (ed.), *Popular Television and Film*, London 1981.

Chapter 5

Altman, D., *The Homosexualization of America*, New York 1982.
Anti-Discriminaton Board of N.S.W., *Discrimination and Homosexuality*, Sydney 1982.
Evans, A., *Witchcraft and the Gay Counter Culture*, Boston 1978.
Fernbach, D., *The Spiral Path*, London 1981.
Foss, P., 'Making Out Love', *Gay Information*, 11, 1982.
Llewellyn-Jones, D., *Everyman*, London 1981.
Rechy, J., *The Sexual Outlaw*, New York 1979.
Royal Commission on Human Relationships, Canberra 1977, 5.
Sheppard, T., *Andrea*, Sydney 1975.
Wilson, P., *The Man They Called a Monster*, Sydney 1981.

Chapter 6

Anderson, J., 'Love and Oppression'., N.S.W.I.T. Paper, 10, 1981.
Brewer, G., *Out of Work, Out of Sight*, Melbourne 1980.
Foucault, M., *The History of Sexuality*, New York 1980.
Lasch, C., *The Culture of Narcissism*, New York 1980.
Moriarty, F., *True Confessions 1919-79*, New York 1979.
Royal Commission on Human Relationships, Canberra, 1977, 3.
Sennett, R., *Authority*, New York 1981.
Slater, P., *Footholds*, New York 1977.
Wilson, P., *Intimacy*, Sydney 1979.

Chapter 7

Australian Consumers Association, *Television Advertising to Children*, Sydney 1982.
Bush, P., *Rape in Australia*, Melbourne 1977.
Carter, A., *The Sadean Woman*, New York 1979.
Faust, B., *Women, Sex and Pornography*, Melbourne 1980.
Royal Commission on Human Relationships, Canberra 1977, 5.
Summers, A., *Damned Whores and God's Police*, Melbourne 1975.
Toner, B., *The Facts of Rape*, London 1977.
Wills, S., 'What Does Pornography Communicate?', unpublished paper, Australian Communications Conference, 1981.
Winnick, C., *Deviance and the Mass Media*, Beverly Hills 1978.
Wilson, P., *The Other Side of Rape*, Brisbane 1978.

Chapter 8

Burns, A., *Breaking Up*, Melbourne 1980.
Conway, R., *Land of the Long Weekend*, Melbourne 1978.
David, D., *The 49% Majority: The Male Sex Role*, New York 1976.

Dinnerstein, D., *The Mermaid and the Minotaur*, New York 1976.
Harper, J., *Fathers at Home*, Melbourne 1980.
Mead, M., *Continuities in Cultural Evolution*, New York 1964.
O'Donnell, J. & Craney, J., *Family Violence in Australia*, Sydney 1981.
Royal Commission on Human Relationships, Canberra 1977, 4.
Williams, C., *Opencut*, Sydney 1981.
Yeatman, A., 'A Sociological View of the Family', in *Children of Parents in Conflict*, Adelaide Dept of Community Welfare, 1979.

Chapter 9

Bednall, D., 'The Family in TV Advertising', *TV Probe*, Sydney 1980.
Chafee, S., *Political Communication*, Beverly Hills 1975.
Edgar, P., *The Unknown Audience*, Melbourne 1979.
Ewen, S., *Captains of Consciousness*, New York 1976.
Fiske, J. & Copping, B., 'An Australian Image of the Monarchy', *Overland*, October 1982.
Goldsen, R., *The Show and Tell Machine*, New York 1977.
Greenberg, B., *Life on Television*, New York 1980.
Wilson, H., 'The Australian *Women's Weekly* 1940-54', N.S.W.I.T. Paper, 15, 1982.

Chapter 10

Monaco, J., *Media Culture*, New York 1978.
Monaco, J., *Celebrity*, New York 1977.
Thomson, D., 'Drugstore Revenge', in Monaco, J., *Celebrity*.

Chapter 11

Bagdikian, B., 'Conglomeration, Concentration, and the Media', *Journal of Communication*, Spring 1980.
Barnouw, E., *The Sponsor*, New York 1978.
Diamond, E., *Good News, Bad News*, Cambridge (U.S.) 1978.
Epstein, E., *News From Nowhere*, New York 1973.
Fiske, J. & Hartley, J., *Reading Television*, London 1978.
Gerbner, G., 'Teacher Image in Mass Culture', in *Communications Technology and Society Policy*, New York 1973.
Glasgow University Media Group, *More Bad News*, London 1980.
Grundy, B., 'Where is the News?', in Edgar, P. (ed.), *The News in Focus*, Melbourne 1980.
Johnson, N., 'Reflections on Australian Broadcasting', Melbourne 1977.
Mattelart, A., *Multinational Systems and the Control of Culture*, Brighton 1979.
Williams, R., *Television: Technology and Cultural Form*, London 1974.

Chapter 12

Benyon, H., *Working For Ford*, London 1973.
Emery, F. & Phillips, C., *Living at Work*, Canberra 1976.
Encel, S., *Equality and Authority*, Melbourne 1970.
Game, A. & Pringle, R., *Gender at Work*, Sydney 1983.
Larson, S., *The Rise of Professionalism*, Berkeley 1977.
Noble, D., *America By Design*, New York 1979.

Noonan, J., *Persons and Masks of the Law*, New York 1976.
Rose, H., *The Political Economy of Science*, London 1976.
Sexton, M. & Maher, L., *The Legal Mystique*, Sydney 1982.
Tomasic, R., *Understanding Lawyers*, Sydney 1978.
Wilkes, J. (ed.), *The Future of Work*, Sydney 1981.

Chapter 13

Curran, J., 'The Impact of Advertising on the British Mass Media', *Media, Culture, and Society*, January 1981.
Downing, J., *The Media Machine*, London 1980.
Higley, J., *Elites in Australia*, London 1979.
Phelan, J., *Mediaworld*, New York 1977.
Radical Education Dossier, 'Education and the Media', Winter, 1981.
Souter, G., *Company of Heralds*, Melbourne 1981.
Speer, G. & Heldorf, P., 'Eyewitness News, Unemployment and Poverty', N.S.W.I.T. Paper, 13, 1982.
Windschuttle, K., *Unemployment*, Melbourne 1980.
Windschuttle, K. & E., *Fixing the News*, Sydney 1981.

Chapter 14

Altheide, D. & Snow, R., *Media Logic*, Beverly Hills 1979.
Bell, P., Boehringer, K. & Crofts, S., *Programmed Politics*, Sydney 1982.
Bonney, B. & Wilson, H., *Australia's Commercial Media*, Melbourne 1983.
Brown, D., *The Prison Struggle*, Melbourne 1982.
Dix, A., 'The ABC in Review', Sydney 1981.
Gans, H., *Deciding What's News*, New York 1979.
Gardner, C. & Young, R., 'Science on Television', in Bennett, T. (ed.), *Popular Television and Film*, London 1981.
Gouldner, A., *The Dialectic of Ideology and Technology*, London 1976.
Hall, S. (et al.), *Policing the Crisis*, London 1978.
Langer, J., 'Television's Personality System', *Media, Culture, and Society*, October 1981.
Noble, G., 'Foreign News in the N.S.W. Media', *Australian Scan*, 10, 1980-1.
Real, M., *Mass Mediated Culture*, New York 1977.
Sargent, M., *Drink and Alcoholism in Australia*, Melbourne 1979.
Sheehy, G., *Passages*, New York 1976.
Whitaker, B., *News Ltd.*, London 1981.

Chapter 15

Altman, D., *Coming Out in the Seventies*, Sydney 1979.
de Beauvoir, S., *Old Age*, London 1977.
Bonney, B., 'Australian Media Ownership and Control', *Media Interventions*, Sydney 1981.
Chessler, P., *About Men*, New York 1978.
Fasteau, M., *The Male Machine*, New York 1974.
Gray, G., *The Warriors*, New York 1967.
Mayer, H., 'Media', in *Australian Politics: a Fifth Reader*, Melbourne 1980.
O'Connor, P., *Understanding the Mid-Life Crisis*, Melbourne 1981.
Spoto, D., *Camerado: Hollywood and the American Man*, New York 1978.
Thomson, D., *America in the Dark*, London 1978.
Tolson, A., *The Limits of Masculinity*, London 1977.

Index

This index is ordered in terms of seven categories: 1 Masculinity
2 Identity 3 Sexuality 4 Media 5 Culture and Communication
6 Places 7 People.

1. MASCULINITY

Male Sex Roles: Heterosexual, 9–14, 82–91, 110, 143–4, 162; Homosexual, 36, 50–9, 61, 68, 90, 116–18, 163, 161, 165; Vocational roles, 11, 12, 13, 125–8; Interpersonal roles, 16, 54, 144–7, 150–3, 162–3.

Negative Interpersonal Behaviour: Alienation, 121–2; Co-option, 162–3; Discrimination, 52; Dominating, 31–2, 100; Double-Bind (paradoxical role injunctions), 84; Doble standard, 61; Distancing, 123–5, 128, 162; Emotional self-repression, 59, 128; Isolating, 155; Manipulating, 29–31, 79; Masking, 126–8, 162.

Male Violence: Aggression, 11, 71, 82–7, 128–8; Emotional violence, 32, 70–1; Domestic violence, 87, 89–91, 97; Modern violence, 10–18, 169; Physical violence, 66, 89, 91, 97, 141, 157–8.

2. IDENTITY

Identity Episodes: Alcoholism, 68, 102; Alienation, 70–1, 61, 121–2; Crime, 87, 97, 98, 133, 157–8; Death, 98, 108, 165*ff*; Militarism, 17–18, 103, 109–19, 158–61; Professionalism, 123–8; Sport, 17, 36–7, 39–49, 87, 103, 116, 149, 161; Strikes, 28, 139–40; Success, 39, 165; Unemployment, 29–31, 68, 123, 136–7, 140; War, 29, 158–61, 159, 166; Women and work, 121–2, 137; Work, 11–13, 122–4, 125–7, 129–42.

3. SEXUALITY

Sexual Episodes: Child-raising, 35, 85, 90–1, 94, 169; Divorce, 82, 88–9; Family Life, 74, 82–9, 93–103; Loneliness, 66–8, 89, 149; Love, 62–5; Prostitution, 62, 72–4; Porn, 62, 75–8; Rape, 23, 33, 78–81, 97; Romance, 63–5, 96.

4. MEDIA

Media Functions: Advice, 98–9; Counselling, 79–80, 99–101; Matchmaking, 35, 66–8; Advertising, 17, 48, 56, 63; Advertising industry, 134–6; Family and, 101–3; Government, 113; Outdoor, 70; Radio, 69, 107, 109; Regulation of, 168–9; Tough men in, 147; Bias, 34, 61–2; Censorship, 31–2, 75; Framing, 62, 92, 113, 115, 116–18, 139; De-contextualization, 140; Displacement, 156; Subliminal association, 93, 109, 148; Influence and ownership, 29, 24, 24–5, 29, 34, 111*ff*, 154–6; Meanings (dominant and secondary), 74, 153–4, 162–3; Provocation, 22–5, 69–71, 81, 107–8, 119, 156–61; Regulation, 55, 56, 77, 135; Stereotyping, 15, 62, 67, 74.

Media Formats

TV Entertainment: *Beauty and the Beast*, 32, 95, 101; *Bandstand*, 114; *Copshop*, 158; *Countdown*, 27; *Mike Walsh Show*, 37, 145.

TV News: *Eyewitness News*, 114, 141; *Four Corners*, 73–4; *Monday Conference*, 114; *Science News*, 119, 152–3; *Sixty Minutes*, 28–9, 112, 114, 148, 166.

TV Soaps: *A Country Practice*, 95, 101, 153; *Sons and Daughters*, 101, 153; *The Sullivans*, 101, 153, 158.

TV Sport: Football, 44–5; Tennis, 41–4; World Series Cricket, 45–7.
Radio: *City Extra*, 73–4; DJ's, 22; Punk, 21, 25; Rock, 21–7, 105–10; *Science Show*, 152; Sports, 49; Talkback, 28–37; Talkback audiences, 30, 33–4, 36, 67, 73, 80, 100.
Newspapers: Fairfax, 29, 33, 56, 95, 155; Financial journalism, 129; Murdoch, 36, 81, 94, 117, 133, 155; Packer, 23, 155; Political journalism, 129, 147; Quality press, 95, 111, 160; Sports journalism, 40, 44, 46–9.
Magazines: *Australian Playboy*, 69, 77, 79, 109; *Bulletin*, 77, 141; *Campaign*, 55; *Penthouse*, 77, 81; *Women's Weekly*, 33, 64, 93.

5. CULTURE AND COMMUNICATION

ABC, 73–4, 114, 116–19, 151, 161, 169
ACA, 76, 102
ADB, 51, 54, 59, 161
Australian identity, 45, 56, 106
Cable TV, 114–5
Celebrity worship, 12, 64, 96, 107–8, 115–16, 130, 153
Children, 70, 76, 78, 102, 112
Communication satellite, 114, 152
Computers, 123–4, 133
Cultural history, 16–17, 66
Cultural narcissism, 53, 70, 77
Cultural reproduction, 1, 78, 83, 86–7, 88–91, 129–30, 162–3
Environment, 34, 150
Feminism, 55, 78, 86, 113
Films: Australian, 9, 55, 64, 68–9, 160; American, 68, 78, 57, 158; Other, 57, 59, 75
Language, 10, 86
Logies, 70
NSW Ombudsman, 157
Religion, 25, 62, 65, 76, 110, 135
Royal Commission on Human Relationships, 51, 52, 59, 71, 89
State Rail Authority, 138–9
Telecom, 138, 139, 152

6. PLACES

America, 23, 34, 48, 65, 83, 86, 97, 105, 108, 113–15, 119, 152, 155–6, 167–8, 173
Brisbane, 26, 97
Britain, 29, 88, 92, 96, 131, 161
China, 167
Falklands, 29, 160
India, 148
Ingham, 81
Melbourne, 21, 73
New Guinea, 107
Paris, 26
Poland, 109, 116, 118
Russia, 116, 118–19, 120
South Africa, 47
Sweden, 152
Sydney, 21, 25, 62, 73, 97, 108, 137
Vietnam, 105

7. PEOPLE

AC/DC, 21, 106
Allen, Peter, 106, 110
Altman, Dennis, 17, 50, 165

Barton, Gordon, 131
Bernstein, Basil, 86
B.H.P., 131, 133–34
Bond, Bruce, 98, 100, 141
Bond, James, 57, 97
Brown, Dave, 157
Buttrose, Ita, 33, 155
Buzo, Alex, 169

Carleton, Richard, 115, 117
Carter, Angela, 75
Casey, Ron, 35, 36, 48
Cash, Pat, 43
de Castella, Robert, 40–1
Cawley, Evonne, 42–3
Chappell, Greg, 46, 47
Charles, Prince, 93–4
Child, Eric, 151
Chessler, Phyllis, 165
Cleary, Michael, 48
Cold Chisel, 28, 106
Collins, Bill (movies), 145–7, 155
Collins, Bill (racing), 48
Connaghan, Terry, 135

Connell, Bob, 141, 155
Conway, Ronald, 83–4
Costigan Inquiry, 133
Crocker, Barry, 110
Cronkite, Walter, 114

Davidson Report, 138
Debray, Regis, 12, 143
Dibble, James, 115, 150–1
Dinnerstein, Dorothy, 90
Duvall, Maureen, 63

Feirstein, Bruce, 169
Fernbach, David, 53, 125
Fiske, John, 93
Fiske, Richard, 49
Fraser, Malcolm, 34, 47, 106, 109, 112, 114

Gibson, Mike, 45
Gilbert, Kevin, 43

Hawke, Robert, 148, 168
Henderson, Brian, 29, 106, 114, 115
Hughes, Kim, 47, 49
Humphries, Barry, 22, 32

Jones, Barry, 121, 168
Jones, Caroline, 116
Jull, David, 134, 148

Kennedy, Graham, 32, 145

Lane, Don, 146
Laws, John, 28–32, 56, 65, 95, 102, 139, 149
Lawson, Henry, 167
Lee, Katrina, 115, 151
Lillee, Dennis, 46
Little River Band, 21, 105
Luger, Milton, 99
Lyn, Vera, 29

May, Norman, 48
Martin, Ray, 149
Mayer, Henry, 112
McEnroe, John, 42–3
McGregor, Craig, 77, 147
McLaren, Father Jim, 80, 100
McLuhan, Marshall, 107
Meldrum, Molly, 21, 27, 145, 146–7, 151
Mills and Boon, 63–4
Moorhouse, Frank, 55
Mossop, Rex, 49, 62

Negus, George, 149
Newcombe, John, 42–3
Neville, Richard, 145
Newton, Bert, 32, 145, 146
Nile, Fred, 36, 58

O'Keefe, Johnny, 106
Olivier, Laurence, 166
Osborne, Clarence, 34

Pacino, Al, 168
Parry-Okeden, Ian, 101
Peacock, Andrew, 94, 111, 34
Pearce, John, 100, 113
Peters, Peter, 49
Porteous, Shane, 150
Price, Ray, 45

Regan, Ronald, 9, 111, 116, 119, 148
Reinecke, Ian, 139
Robertson, Clive, 95, 151
Robinson, Peter, 147

Selleck, Tom, 145
Sheehy, Gail, 143
Singleton, John, 28, 29, 56, 66–67, 100, 110
Stone, Gerald, 114
de Stoop, Micki, 33, 136, 147
Symonds, Ross, 114, 115
Symons, Red, 58

Thatcher, Margaret, 3, 18, 148
Thomson, David, 166
Throsby, Margaret, 37, 73–4, 100, 151
Tingle, John, 28, 33–5, 101, 147, 150
Tresizes, Neil, 48

Walsh, Mike, 37, 145–6, 155
Warhol, Andy, 110
Whitlam, Gough, 88, 92
Willesee, Mike, 36, 66, 114
Williams, Clare, 86
Williams, Robin, 152
Williamson, David, 161
Wilson, Paul, 54, 65, 78
Wiltshire, Brian, 66–67
Windschuttle, Keith, 139
Wright, Dr James, 99, 100, 145

Yeatman, Anna, 82, 84

Zavros, Spiro, 140